EDUCATIONAL ADMINISTRATION

HOW TO ORDER THIS BOOK

BY PHONE: 800-233-9936 or 717-291-5609, 8AM–5PM Eastern Time

BY FAX: 717-295-4538

BY MAIL: Order Department
Technomic Publishing Company, Inc.
851 New Holland Avenue, Box 3535
Lancaster, PA 17604, U.S.A.

BY CREDIT CARD: American Express, VISA, MasterCard

PERMISSION TO PHOTOCOPY–POLICY STATEMENT

Authorization to photocopy items for internal or personal use, or the internal or personal use of specific clients, is granted by Technomic Publishing Co., Inc. provided that the base fee of US $3.00 per copy, plus US $ .25 per page is paid directly to Copyright Clearance Center, 222 Rosewood Drive, Danvers, MA 01923, USA. For those organizations that have been granted a photocopy license by CCC, a separate system of payment has been arranged. The fee code for users of the Transactional Reporting Service is 1-56676/94 $5.00 + $ .25.

Educational Administration: Inquiry Values Practice

REVISED EDITION

Donald J. Willower
The Pennsylvania State University

LANCASTER · BASEL

Educational Administration
a **TECHNOMIC**® publication

Published in the Western Hemisphere by
Technomic Publishing Company, Inc.
851 New Holland Avenue, Box 3535
Lancaster, Pennsylvania 17604 U.S.A.

Distributed in the Rest of the World by
Technomic Publishing AG
Missionsstrasse 44
CH-4055 Basel, Switzerland

Copyright © 1994 by Technomic Publishing Company, Inc.
All rights reserved

No part of this publication may be reproduced, stored in a
retrieval system, or transmitted, in any form or by any means,
electronic, mechanical, photocopying, recording, or otherwise,
without the prior written permission of the publisher.

Printed in the United States of America
10 9 8 7 6 5 4 3 2 1

Main entry under title:
 Educational Administration: Inquiry, Values, Practice — Revised Edition

A Technomic Publishing Company book
Bibliography: p.
Includes index p. 83

Library of Congress Catalog Card No. 94-61184
ISBN No. 1-56676-215-4

TABLE OF CONTENTS

Preface to the Revised Edition vii
Preface to the First Edition ix
Introduction xi

1. A BRIEF EXCURSION INTO RECENT HISTORY   1

   The Social Sciences: Variety, Tough-Mindedness,
      Specialization 2
   The Social Sciences Reproached: (at Least) Two
      Renderings 4
   Reactions and Criticisms 16

2. RECONSTRUCTING THE FUTURE   21

   Advocacy, Confusion, Invigoration 22
   Inquiry 24
   Values 32
   Praxis 38
   Professing 44

3. CONCLUDING COMMENTS   59

Endnotes 61
Bibliographic Addendum 81
Index 83
About the Author 85

v

PREFACE TO THE REVISED EDITION

EDUCATIONAL Administration: Inquiry, Values, Practice is the retitled revised edition of the monograph originally published by the National Council of Professors of Educational Administration as *Educational Administration: Philosophy, Praxis, Professing*.

This edition has a number of improvements. There is a Table of Contents and an Index. This makes the book easier to use in graduate classes where professors and students may wish to emphasize particular topics. For example, some have been especially interested in the historical treatment of the turn toward the social sciences in educational administration, critical theory, subjectivism, and alternatives to the latter two perspectives. Others have focused on the sections on values and reflective practice. Still others have chosen to stress the conception of inquiry presented in the monograph. A bibliographic addendum composed of citations to and comments on some relevant work appearing since the first edition now follows the endnotes.

I am delighted that Technomic Publishing Company has decided to publish this new edition. Thanks are due my colleague at Penn State, Paula M. Short, who as NCPEA president arranged the publication of the new edition by Technomic Publishing Company, publisher of the NCPEA Yearbook series. I am also grateful to Joseph L. Eckenrode of Technomic who holds a Ph.D. in philosophy and felt the monograph deserved a wider audience. I am pleased, too, that the NCPEA connection remains strong and that royalties go to that organization, which has done so much to advance educational administration as a field of study and practice.

DONALD J. WILLOWER

PREFACE TO THE FIRST EDITION

WHEN Paul Bredeson asked if I would present NCPEA's Cocking Lecture, I was interested for a number of reasons, both personal and professional. I remember Walter Cocking from my doctoral student days at The University of Buffalo (now State University of New York at Buffalo). A tall, imposing figure, rarely without a cigar, Cocking came to Buffalo from time to time and visited with George Holloway, who headed Buffalo's educational administration program and the Western New York School Study Council and for whom I worked in both units during my two years of residence at the University. Cocking and Holloway would exchange stories and strategies often connected with groups like NCPEA, the American Association of School Administrators, and the Collegiate Association for the Development of Educational Administration (a state-level professors' organization) for which Holloway served as president. On Holloway's advice, I first attended NCPEA in 1958. Another important link to NCPEA was Robert Fisk, Dean of the School of Education and my academic advisor. Fisk had served as NCPEA chairman in 1953 and was a contributor to the landmark book on administrative behavior edited by Campbell and Gregg, which it sponsored. In addition, NCPEA held its 1959 meeting at the University. I graduated and had accepted a position at Penn State starting in the fall but stayed on in Buffalo to teach summer session. As it turned out, I also helped with NCPEA arrangements and made a presentation in the group on theory chaired by Dan Griffiths. I attended NCPEA for the third time in 1960, but Penn State had changed its calendar making it difficult to go, and when a 1984 change made it possible again, I used the time for other pursuits. I did feel guilty, however, given the organization's importance and my early participation.

On the professional side, I felt that the ongoing intellectual debates in the field had often mystified, rather than enlightened, and had contributed to a widening separation of theory and practice. Since I had extensive preparation in philosophy and sociology, I thought I might be able to put some of the issues in perspective. I also wanted to present a constructive view that would recognize the potentially symbiotic relationship of theory and practice.

As Paul and I talked about the project, it eventually became clear that such topics required a longer piece than would normally constitute a Cocking Lecture. NCPEA was interested in reviving its monograph series, and it was finally decided that I should prepare a lengthy document. The Cocking Lecture was to become a precis.

So the summer of 1991 became our NCPEA summer. The monograph was been a major preoccupation since the end of the spring semester and I no longer feel any guilt about NCPEA!

In addition to Paul Bredeson, three people have been especially helpful. Bill Caldwell, our department head, has been consistently interested and supportive. Judy Leonard managed the production of the manuscript with her usual combination of high competence and geniality. My wife Catherine, a constant source of inspiration and good counsel, created at home the best possible conditions for work, often doing my share of our common chores as well as her own.

DONALD J. WILLOWER

INTRODUCTION

EDUCATIONAL administration as a field of study has undergone a variety of changes over the years. Some have had widespread support, and some have been accompanied by considerable debate. More recently, the conflict level has been high as differing views have been advanced about what inquiry should be and how it should be conducted. Such questions go beyond issues of strategies in theorizing and research. They have a philosophic side since they can be tied to competing epistemological positions and different values.

Intellectual trends in the field tend to reflect those in the various disciplines that undergird educational administration, although the reflection is far from perfect since every area of scholarship has its own special problems and peculiarities. I will examine those trends as they have been played out in educational administration. Then I will explore future possibilities, presenting ideas that I believe could usefully inform both inquiry and practice. Finally, special attention will be given to issues in professing educational administration.

Two key ideas will, I hope, become apparent. One is that many of the intellectual issues in educational administration, especially those that fuel the debates in the field, cannot be understood in black and white terms. Although they have often been portrayed that way by adherents of one ideology or another or by the uninformed, they are often gray in this realm, just as they are in the practice of administration. Put differently, things are usually more complicated than they seem at first. The other is that despite the controversies and the complexities inherent in educational administration, the field is vibrant, exciting, and full of challenges and possibilities.

CHAPTER 1

A Brief Excursion into Recent History

IN the 1950s, educational administration, as taught and studied in universities, began to put more emphasis on the social sciences as sources of relevant concepts and theories. The reasoning was straightforward. Educational administrators' work took place in formal and informal groups and organizations. Administrators were expected to attend to motivation and morale within their organizations, to articulate purposes, and to take some responsibility for outcomes. They frequently coped with conflict and power figures and groups, both internally and in the community. On a daily basis they faced decisions that required choices among courses of action reflecting competing values. It was obvious that educational administration was substantively concerned with topics that had been, and were, the objects of relatively sustained investigation in the social sciences and philosophy as well, and it made sense to seek whatever insights were available. These insights could be incorporated into preparation programs in educational administration, but there was another benefit: The conceptual and methodological resources of the various disciplines could be tapped to advance inquiry in educational administration.

This broadening of the intellectual focus of the field was one aspect of a larger effort to improve and professionalize graduate study and scholarship in educational administration that gained impetus in the 1950s and has continued in various guises to the present. Major players in the early days included the Kellogg Foundation, which provided financial support; the Cooperative Program in Educational Administration, the Committee for the Advancement of School Administration of the American Association of School Administrators, the National Conference, now Council, of Professors of Educational Administration and the University Council for Educational Administration.[1] Today, some of the issues and some of the players have changed, but the point is that in the 1950s there was strong support from diverse groups for a more sophisticated, more scientific grounding for educational administration.

THE SOCIAL SCIENCES: VARIETY, TOUGH-MINDEDNESS, SPECIALIZATION

The effort to ground educational administration in the social sciences set the stage for several decades of scholarship. Facilitated by the appearance in the 1960s of two new journals, The *Journal of Educational Administration* and *Educational Administration Quarterly,* and by numerous conferences and programs devoted to theoretical and research themes and issues, a wide variety of scholarly writing was produced.[2] The empirical work was largely quantitative, often employing paper and pencil instruments as measures of variables whose relationships were under investigation. However, there were also a fair number of field studies that employed participant observation or ethnographic-type methods, beginning with Boyan's examination of the social system of a junior high school in 1951, and there were numerous calls during the 1950s and 1960s for more of this type of research.[3]

My recollections of the twenty years beginning in the mid to late 1950s are of a time of productivity and progress in inquiry in educational administration. Our understanding of schools was deepened by seeing them as complex organizations, which were also socio-cultural systems made up of diverse and often divergent adult and student groups; a greater appreciation was gained of the importance of school climates and leadership that stressed both colleagueship and goal attainment; and we became more knowledgeable about the political and economic contexts of education, which in the first case was concerned with governance, power, special interests, and the competition for resources, and in the second, equity and the relation of allocations and outcomes. The insights that accompanied this activity often took the form of new concepts and embryonic middle-range theories or explanations covering quite limited sets of phenomena.[4] The picture was clearly one of conceptual pluralism. No one framework held sway over the others, even within the field's various specialties. Much of the work used ideas borrowed from the social sciences. In fact, a number of books were published that attempted to examine systematically the contributions that the various social sciences might make in understanding the administration of schools.[5] The whole array of social sciences—sociology, political science, anthropology, psychology, and economics—was tapped.

The multiple ways of seeing the world of educational administration available from these sources enlarged vision by furnishing new ideas but could also be overwhelming. Relevance became a key issue, and much was written about what the special circumstances of educational administration required.[6] Thoughtful questions about the uses and limitations of the social sciences were raised from the beginning. Nor were values and philosophy ignored. The landmark 1957 book *Administrative Behavior in Education,* which was sponsored by NCPEA, contained a lengthy chapter on values and many other works on values and philosophy were published and conferences on these topics were scheduled during the time when enthusiasm in educational administration for the social sciences was especially strong.[7]

The twenty years following 1957 were marked by a diversity of activities, interests, and viewpoints in educational administration. For instance, a great deal of energy went into issues connected with preparation programs as a wide array of instructional materials, including simulations and case studies and a variety of approaches from using the novel in teaching administration to the creation of more effective internships, were developed.[8] The topic of common and specialized learnings for administrators in different kinds of positions, both within educational administration and across types of organizations, received much attention.[9]

Without belaboring it further, the point is that educational administration was anything but a single-minded enterprise during the ascendancy of the social sciences. Variety was the rule: no one social science, theory, or methodology dominated and professors were interested in an assortment of activities, as they are today. Some were especially oriented to teaching, advising, and curriculum; some spent large amounts of time working with schools and school systems, and some did research. However, substantive, continuing scholarship was the province of limited numbers.[10]

Nevertheless, those who did the research and writing produced the literature of educational administration, which, in turn, became the basis for the field's textbooks[11] and the subject matter of much of what was taught to prospective school administrators. And the bulk of the work was done in the style and manner of one or another of the social sciences. Educational administration was ready for this because of the obvious relevance of much social science to the field and because of the hope that a more substantive understanding of schools would lead to their improvement. Further, there was a widespread feeling that the literature of educational administration was hortatory, imprecise, and too often based on the pontifications of "great men."[12] Science, after all, put everyone on a more equal footing. Even the pronouncements of "great men" could be critically examined for the logic of their reasoning and their fit to relevant data.

The turn toward more scientific thinking in educational administration brought what science normally confers: an array of diverse concepts, theories, and methodologies that could be used in the study of educational institutions, and legitimation for more probing, more critical, and tougher-minded modes of communication. Much good work came from this (and continues to be done) although various critics from time to time pointed to limitations, often from the perspective of methodological rigor.[13]

An additional consequence was the development of greater faculty diversity in educational administration in the form of new specializations. Some, such as politics of education and economics of education, fitted one of the social sciences while others such as organizational studies were more interdisciplinary, drawing from sociology, psychology, and certain applied fields like business administration that used the rubric of administrative science.[14] Such diversity led to a certain fragmentation as each specialty has its particular interests, its own (often competing) theories and methods, and even its own languages.[15]

While professors of educational administration were employing a variety of concepts, theories, and methods from the social sciences in their scholarship and while faculty were becoming more tough-minded and more specialized, the social sciences themselves began to undergo changes. The 1960s and 1970s were a time marked by disillusionment and a distrust of societal institutions. Government, technology, science, and sundry economic and social arrangements became targets of disapproval and protest. Students and professors, especially in the social and humanistic disciplines, were among the most vocal participants. Their activism, along with that of other groups interested in social change, helped to foster the spread of perspectives that were highly critical of, among other things, social science.

THE SOCIAL SCIENCES REPROACHED: (AT LEAST) TWO RENDERINGS

Critics attacked what they perceived to be dominant thinking in the social sciences. Proponents of two quite dissimilar points of view, neo-Marxism and subjectivism, led the assault.[16] Each of these views had longstanding roots in philosophy and the social sciences but, until the 1960s and 1970s, had been quite marginal in both places. However, spurred by the spirit of the times, especially as it was manifested on the campuses, both perspectives took hold in most of the social and humanistic disciplines and eventually entered the literature of educational administration. Ironically, the criticisms of science that were advanced in educational administration underscored that field's connections to the social sciences: these criticisms faithfully mirrored those that had occurred in the social sciences themselves.[17]

For decades, Marxists articulated a critique of the social sciences tied to their views of unjust arrangements and lopsided distributions of power in capitalist societies, while subjectivists, sometimes using other labels, questioned what they saw as the overly objectified, dehumanizing features of science. Today, in a time Wallerstein calls "the era of a thousand Marxisms,"[18] the versions of that perspective range from orthodox to critical theory to analytic Marxism.[19] Subjectivistic views in the social sciences are usually thought to stem from philosophical idealism or, especially in more recent years, from phenomenology or existentialism. In sociology, Alfred Schutz's work and the ethnomethodology of Garfinkel are usually labeled phenomenological while such writers as Manning have explored existential sociology.[20] Symbolic interactionism, often claimed by subjectivists, is a less clear case since its chief forebear is G. H. Mead, a pragmatist philosopher, and Blumer, perhaps its leading sociological advocate, appears to have rejected philosophical subjectivism, according to Smelser.[21] In any event, these approaches tend to be sympathetic to interpretive and hermeneutic methods.

The neo-Marxist and subjectivist camps in the social sciences exhibit the same internal diversity characteristic of other general orientations. Just as the various, usually more scientific, perspectives in the social sciences are multivoiced, so it is with neo-Marxism and subjectivism. Furthermore, these two views have been strongly opposed to each other in philosophy over the years and, despite some similarities in connection with their criticisms of science, they remain fundamentally different within the social sciences. Marxists employ macro units like societies and social classes in their analyses and tend to accept structuralist thinking. In contrast, subjectivists look to such micro units as individuals and their interactions with one another and typically emphasize the social construction and negotiation of reality. Both have distinctive normative interests: The former stresses societal change through conflict and class struggle, while the latter is concerned with the interplay of individual values and social pressures and its effects for those involved.

Another complication is that various groups and individuals may share one or a few views or interests of neo-Marxists or subjectivists, but not much else. For instance, feminists advocate societal change as do Marxists, emphasizing gender instead of social class, but the positions of feminist scholars on neo-Marxism run the gamut from strong support to outright rejection. Another example is the classic work of W. Lloyd Warner and his colleagues on social class. They shared a vital interest in that topic with Marxists but came at it from an entirely different point of view. Still another example is found in the numerous studies that document the trials and tribulations of individuals in various social settings, often using case study or ethnographic methods, which are not connected to the subjectivist critique. After all, many scholars simply conduct their research without paying much attention to broader schools of thought, unconcerned about whether their interests happen to coincide with those of one or another of these schools.

Despite all these crosscurrents and complexities, discernible versions of neo-Marxist and subjectivist scholarship have gained considerable prominence in the educational administration literature. Critical theory has perhaps been the leading form of neo-Marxism reflected in that literature, and the work of T. B. Greenfield and his supporters has been the chief version of subjectivism.

Critical Theory

Called by one of its historians "a 'school' of Western Marxism,"[22] critical theory had its origins in the Institute of Social Research founded in Frankfurt in 1923. Referred to as the Frankfurt School after its return in 1950 to that city following a sojourn at Columbia University during the Nazi period and war years, this version of neo-Marxian thought found expression in the work of Horkheimer, Adorno, and Marcuse, among others. Its best known later figure is Jürgen Habermas. A pivotal project of the Frankfurt School was the reinterpretation of Marxism to account for historical trends that did not fit Marx's predictions. Put differently, it was the renovation of Marxist thought in the light of modern societal and technological development.

Capitalism in the Western democracies was softened by reforms that at least partially regulated the economic system in the public interest, and workers in those countries lacked class consciousness. This lack and the acceptance of the status quo that it implied was labeled false consciousness, which became a key concept for critical theorists. The general idea was that the development of false consciousness rather than class consciousness, was engineered by the ruling classes. This was accomplished through subtle mechanisms of control that were institutionalized in schools, the workplace, the mass media, entertainment and recreation, patterns of consumption, and other societal arrangements. Not least among them was science which was depicted as serving the interests of the dominant classes despite its claims to objectivity. Thus, criticism of social institutions and class-based patterns of domination and oppression became a central concern of critical theorists.

In education, neo-Marxist writing has, in the past, been found mainly in the foundations areas. The so-called new sociology of education in Great Britain, for example, produced much work in this tradition (as well as some that is harder to classify).[23] However, in educational administration, as in some other areas of education, neo-Marxism did not enter the mainstream literature in a serious way until the 1980s.

Three features of the neo-Marxist critique in education and educational administration will be considered. One deals with science, one with schools as societal institutions, and one with the role of educators and the schools in social change.

Science and Repression

Although orthodox Marxists were fond of terms like *scientific socialism* or *dialectical science*, they defined *science* in a special way. Most critical theorists emphasized the consequences of science as a societally controlled institution but also subscribed to the Marxian epistemology. Horkheimer, for instance, contended that verification was not a matter of experiments or documentation, but of "historical struggles, in which conviction itself plays an essential role."[24] However, some neo-Marxists, such as Gouldner, emphasized that theories can have liberating or repressive consequences but readily conceded that validation is not determined by those consequences.

For most critical theorists ideological argumentation is more important than empirical documentation, and there is wide mistrust and sometimes outright rejection of scientific norms. Attacks on science sometimes depict the physical and life sciences as catspaws of commercial and economic circles and the social sciences as mystifiers of social relations.

In educational administration, Foster drew on critical theory, especially the work of Habermas, and rejected scientific approaches to administration. He argued that the normative role of school administrators should be stressed, especially in connection with relations of social class and power that block the realization of equal opportunity. In Foster's view, this normative role is ignored by administrative science, exemplified by writers such as Herbert Simon.[25] Bates, citing sources in the new sociology of education, contended that ideology influences science: social and economic forces control how knowledge is defined, organized, and transmitted. He argued that organizations such as schools regulate access to knowledge in ways that favor some groups and exclude others and asserted that school administrators abet or cope with this situation rather than attempt to change it.[26]

Critical theorists contend that the very theories used to examine schools and schooling function to legitimate current inequitable arrangements and practices. Positivism and functionalism are often their main targets in this connection. The former is committed to science at the expense of values; the latter sustains the status quo.[27]

Although neo-Marxists are generally suspicious of empirical science, and most of their writing is in the form of argument and sometimes polemics, there is an empirical literature as well. A contemporary example is critical ethnography. Done within the Marxian ideological framework, this scholarship is explicit about its primary objective, which is social change.[28] Usually, such studies emphasize the societal context of schooling.

Schools as Societal Institutions

Much recent empirical work has dealt with reproduction and resistance. In the neo-Marxist literature on schooling, reproduction refers to the perpetuation of current societal relationships and conditions. Put somewhat simplistically, schooling reproduces the status quo. This, of course, is hardly a unique idea. It is found in institutional theory in education and in the writing of a host of sociologists from Waller to the present, since education in every kind of society inculcates values and beliefs as part of the processes of socialization.[29] The special twist provided by critical theorists and other neo-Marxists is an emphasis on social class and economic forces. They believe that the schools promote the interests of the dominant classes at the expense of the underclasses. According to their analysis, this is accomplished not only as a result of the content of the curriculum and the nature of the norms taught in schools, but also because of the sorting of students into channels that lead to different occupational categories.

Reproduction theory has been criticized because it offers little hope for change.[30] Hence, some studies have examined resistance to reproductive forces in schools. One of the best of these was done by Willis.[31] His book illustrates the blend of field data and social commentary found in neo-Marxist empirical studies. Willis showed how the working class values of the small group of boys he observed in an English school led them to reject academics and conformity to the language, manners, and beliefs imposed by the school. Instead, they pursued their interests in material things, girls, and real work. Willis underscored what he saw as a dilemma for working class youth: by resisting the school's requirements, they forfeited the opportunities for upward mobility that education could provide.

Despite studies such as this one, which can serve as a prototype for critical ethnographies, neo-Marxist literature in education, as elsewhere, remains largely and steadfastly non-empirical. Indeed, field research has been subordinated to social criticism in Marxism from the beginning to the present time.

Educators, Schools, and Social Change

In the light of its emphasis on the necessity of overturning oppressive societal arrangements, the critical theorists' conception of social change becomes paramount. The orthodox Marxist theory of revolution grounded in a dialectical interpretation of history, with all its failed predictions, now appears dead. In any event, critical theorists are oriented to critical analysis, resistance, and radical reform — not revolution. Marxists took the term *praxis* from philosophy where it was usually employed as an equivalent for thoughtful practice. They used it to refer to practice or political action on behalf of Marxian goals.

Critical theory has been reproved by orthodox Marxists for being too devoted to theoretical disquisition and not enough to praxis.[32] It is true that critical theorists undertook elaborate analyses of social institutions. Furthermore, once the simplistic slogans of revolution were discarded by most modern Marxists, the search for appropriate mechanisms of social change proved complex, resulting in little that could be described as agreed upon programs. The strong suit of critical theory and of neo-Marxism in general remains its largely negative assessment of societal institutions. Praxis continues to be a goal, but it seems to be defined mainly in terms of getting involved in activities that are consistent with Marxist ideals such as the emancipation of those oppressed by dominative social structures.

A special problem for critical theorists is the issue of fundamental versus superficial change. Some of them see representative democracy as essentially corrupt and liberalism as an enemy because of what they regard as its band-aid solutions to social problems. Their dilemma is that calls for fundamental change would probably erode what little public support they may have, making such change even more unlikely, while calls for incremental change both deny their ideology and seem likely to decrease their already very limited role as a distinct political force.

In any case, critical theorists in education have not gone far beyond criticism. One monograph titled *Critical Theory and Educational Practice* is strong on the former and weak on the latter: It is essentially a scholarly treatment of three figures of the Frankfurt School, along with a brief discussion of a radical pedagogy that would require new languages, values, and practices yet to be fashioned.[33] Indeed, it is hard to find amidst the indictments of schools and school administrators set forth by critical theorists, writing about positive reform.

One of the more specific efforts along these lines focused primarily on teachers and teacher education, but its implications for administration can be readily discerned.[34] This essay, by Giroux and McLaren, begins with a recognition of the failure of "leftist educators" to go beyond critique. Such educators have theorized *about* schools rather than *for* schools. What is needed, the authors contend, is education that produces radicalized teachers (or administrators) who work in the interest of an "emancipatory vision." This means intellectuals "willing to play a central role in the broad struggle for democracy and social justice."[35] To do so, they need to be able to analyze entrenched relations of power in schools as reflected in texts, curricula, and other practices and policies and to develop ways of participating in social struggles aimed at the achievement of genuinely democratic schools. Their preparation must be recast as a form of "cultural politics" so that, as educators, they will foster student knowledge and skills "necessary to struggle toward the realization of a more just and human world."[36]

Such recommendations are consistent with critical theorists' nonrevolutionary conception of praxis: political action in the service of social justice in the school setting and in broader arenas. Undergirding this would be educator preparation programs that accommodate neo-Marxist objectives.

Subjectivism

Phenomenology, existentialism, and most forms of idealism in philosophy look inward to the mind rather than outward to the world. They attempt to understand or intuit reality primarily through various methods of thinking or reasoning, hence the terms *phenomenological analysis, hermeneutics,* or more broadly, *interpretive methods.*

Such methods commonly have been given distinctive forms. For example, Husserl, the founder of phenomenology, specifically described phenomenological methods. A principal feature was the effort to set aside or bracket all presuppositions in order to penetrate to the essence of the concept under analysis.[37] Hermeneutics, the science of interpretation, goes back to ancient Greek attempts to decipher the meaning of poetry. It later became a subfield of theology because of the importance of understanding scriptural texts. Eventually resecularized, especially through the work of philosophers such as Dilthey, hermeneutics now has gained greater recognition in philosophy and some of the social sciences.[38] The term usually refers to the explication of meaning by examining language, contexts, and other sources but increasingly has been used more broadly in this literature, often synonymously with reflective exposition. Vandenberg, for instance, in an explicitly intended phenomenological analysis of the school as an educational institution called his effort hermeneutical phenomenology.[39]

An important element in phenomenological and hermeneutical applications to the social sciences was the significance of empathic understanding for meaningful interpretation, a point found, for example, in Dilthey. Early phenomenological analyses in sociology, such as those of Alfred Vierkandt and Max Scheler, explored such fundamental dispositions as sympathy, sociability, self-respect, and imitation as well as collective phenomena like morale, group self-consciousness, and cultural axioms.[40] Later versions of phenomenological sociology did not follow a single path. Heap and Roth identified four types of phenomenological thought in sociology and dismissed several others as using the concepts of phenomenology only metaphorically.[41]

Hence, a crucial question to ask of phenomenological approaches in the social sciences is whether they are grounded in philosophical phenomenology, that is, in the methods of Husserl, or if they use the label more loosely, for example, to indicate the significance of subjective meaning in social relations. The looser usage is increasingly found in the social sciences and especially in applied areas like education, business, or communications. Some careful writers explicitly state that their work is not to be confused with Husserl's philosophy and some commentators use phrases like *phenomenological in orientation* or *spirit* to refer to scholarship that emphasizes subjectivity.[42]

Related in a general way to phenomenologically based or oriented strands of thought in the social sciences are those that are existentialist in character, some that label themselves humanistic psychology or sociology, and the symbolic interactionists, among others. These perspectives often differ on important points, for example, the emphasis given to introspection or to inter-subjectivity, and there are individualized accounts of each perspective. The point to keep in mind is that it is simply incorrect to see the social sciences as comprising only one or a few theoretical approaches.[43] Even within broad schools of thought there are subtypes and frequent disputes.

In educational administration, Hartley proposed in 1970 that a subjectivistic philosophy, humanistic existentialism, was appropriate for the field,[44] but the subjectivist position has been developed most notably in the writings of one person, T. B. Greenfield. Originally an advocate of systems theory, since the mid-1970s Greenfield has been a critic of science and the leading proponent of subjectivism in educational administration.[45] Three aspects of this work will be considered: Greenfield's attack on science, his concerns about values, and the relationship of subjectivism to empirical studies in educational administration.

Attack on Science

Greenfield's critique of science took the form of a general criticism of science and positivism, which he equated, and a more specific one of quantitative studies in educational administration. His views have been framed throughout by what he perceived as a dichotomized intellectual world. In one paper he wrote of "two fundamentally different ways of looking at the world" and ten years later he opened a review of literature with the statement that "theorists take one of two positions when they speak of organizations."[46] The two views are positivistic science on the one side and the subjectivism that he has adopted on the other.

He argued that science shuts out and disallows any other ways of knowing: there is no place in science for values, for feelings, for wisdom. A scientistic point of view, he contended, dominates thought and research in administration, a condition he attributed largely to the influence of Herbert Simon. Greenfield described the positivistic science he opposed as holding that "only that which is quantifiable and calculable is real, for that is the only kind of reality consistent with the limited rationality that finds its ultimate expression in the linear workings of computers."[47] In common with the Marxists, he sees reification in social science: concepts such as organization give to those collectivities the status of entities, which makes them more, and more important and powerful, than the individuals who compose them. Administrative science is cut off from the realities of administrative life, the world of individual values, motives, commitments, and conflict. This, Greenfield believes, fits the view administrators want to have of themselves, that is, as objective and rational. However, the administrator in this science emerges as a devalued, dehumanized technocrat.

All of this was accepted in educational administration, Greenfield averred, when that field embraced the social sciences. It was especially reflected in the systems thinking and quantitative research that social science fostered. Both promoted an emphasis on efficiency and effectiveness to the detriment of moral concerns. Most of the research in educational administration is, for Greenfield, irrelevant because it fails to deal with such matters as will, intention, freedom, and compulsion. The kind of research Greenfield proposed asks such questions as how and by whom the social reality of organizations is built, what part language plays in administrative life, and what constitutes good and right administrative action in the context of specific educational issues. The preferred style of research is qualitative for Greenfield who cited as exemplars a number of studies of that kind.[48]

Values

The importance of values is one of Greenfield's key themes. It appears often in his published papers, usually as part of his critique of science. His main point has been that science is exclusively devoted to the descriptive while the main issues in administration are normative. He has not gone beyond this to develop a theory of ethical choice or a conception of values. He does, however, cite Hodgkinson approvingly in this connection. Hodgkinson's treatment of values is quite well developed and is specifically applied to administration. In addition, it appears to be generally consistent with the kind of subjectivism Greenfield has adopted. Hodgkinson set forth a hierarchical conception of values.[49] It consisted of three levels based on whether values are grounded by personal preferences, appeals to reason, or principles that have a quality of absoluteness. The latter are at the highest level of the hierarchy and are tied to commitment and belief. Personal preferences, the lowest level, are ubiquitous but often organizationally constrained, and at the middle level, appeals to reason, in the form of both analysis and consensus shaping, are common administrative activities. While this perspective has been criticized because of the potential competition among values, all of which have the status of principles,[50] it remains a good example of an effort to examine values more systematically. This seems essential, especially for a point of view that emphasizes values as a critically important aspect of educational administration.

Empirical Studies

There is no equivalent to critical ethnography in subjectivism in educational administration. Field studies are common, but few identify themselves as subjectivist researchers. Blase, who has done a number of excellent observational-interview studies, has recently begun to identify himself with symbolic interactionism, but, as noted earlier, that perspective has only one foot in the subjectivist camp.[51] Greenfield has produced little empirical work since his systems theory days and field researchers rarely tie their work to his views, so making a direct connection between an ethnographic-type study and his form of subjectivism is difficult. Nor can it be argued that all field research is grounded in subjectivism since such researchers might reject that view and some are committed to field work that strives to be as rigorous as possible.[52] After all, field studies can have many purposes from empathetic understanding to hypothesis development or even testing, and they are compatible with a variety of philosophical and social science orientations. At the same time, it is obvious that the depth of the data on individuals and their social contexts generated in qualitative research is of special interest from a subjectivist point of view, and it is no doubt the case that Greenfield's writing has helped to stimulate this kind of research in educational administration.

Examples of field work that seem close to the spirit of subjectivism are autobiographical accounts like Hart's efforts to make sense of her experiences as a new school principal and highly interpretive portrayals of administrators at work such as Gronn's analysis of conversations.[53] These kinds of studies seek to provide an emic perspective, that of the person who is the subject of the investigation. The importance of the views of those studied is also underscored by the increasing popularity of asking subjects to read and comment on drafts of ethnographic narratives in which they figure. Such ways of giving voice to individuals appear especially to fit subjectivist thinking.

Overall, it seems fair to conclude that the trend toward field research in educational administration[54] (and education generally) is too multi-faceted to attribute to any one movement, theory, or philosophical point of view. Subjectivism has been one contributing factor among others, and the same can be said of critical theory. In any case, the relationship between subjectivism and empirical studies in educational administration is neither direct nor clear. Interestingly and possibly influenced by Greenfield's attacks on quantitative studies, there is no effort to do quantitative research on subjectivist themes, as Adorno did for critical theory with the development and use of the famous F Scale.[55]

Other Forces

A number of other intellectual forces have facilitated or directly contributed to the critique of science. Some of them are broad and probably helped bring about the spread of the two perspectives just considered. Kuhn's history of what he called paradigm shifts in the physical sciences showed that new theory was often adopted as a result of changing social and intellectual contexts, not because the old theory was disproved. Other ideas such as Heisenberg's uncertainty principle and chaos theory have been routinely invoked in opposition to scientific determinism. Postmodernism, characterized by an emphasis on indeterminacy, the distrust of reason, and the deconstruction of ideas, has become fashionable in some social sciences and even more so in the humanities, especially in fields like literary criticism that do not have strong traditions of rigorous scholarship. Having some philosophical ties to Nietzsche, it is represented in the work of Derrida, Foucault, and Lyotard, among others.[56] Highly relativistic, postmodernism is closer to subjectivism than to critical theory, which is usually classified as modernist because of its belief in a meaningful and perfectible world. In any case, postmodernism's anti-rational and anti-systems predilections make it critical of science and its modes of discourse, as well as of most forms of organization and administration.[57] Although a few writers use the term *deconstruction* to refer to their critical analyses, postmodernism has not yet had a noteworthy impact in the literature of educational administration.

Much more important there (and in education generally) have been strands of scholarship devoted to studying and improving the circumstances of certain categories of people; this writing has been primarily on gender, race, and ethnicity.[58] It has been reformist in orientation, seeking social justice and greater voice for its constituencies. Criticisms of science have ranged from those that point to subtle biases or lacunae in social science concepts and theories all the way to those that suggest different or separate science for particular groups. Feminism currently appears to be the strongest of these strands of thought, at least in educational administration.

All of these forces have abetted and added to the critique of science led in the universities by critical theorists and subjectivists. An often unrecognized additional element has been that scholars in the social sciences and in educational administration who were committed to science, but not to scientism or positivism, have also been critical. They have been concerned about the knowledge for what question, the separation of science from humanistic thought and values, the commercialization of science and its attendant grantsmanship, over-quantification and the use of complex regimens to study insignificant problems, and the failure of much research to connect to the realities of work and life.[59]

REACTIONS AND CRITICISMS

Some of the points made by critical theorists and subjectivists were noncontroversial and already well accepted in educational administration, but others drew fire. Examples of the former were the importance of values in administration and the utility of ethnographic-style research. Values were accepted virtually everywhere as central to administrative choice, and qualitative studies were widely seen as getting at the realities of school life in ways that questionnaires did not. The disagreements ranged over a wide array of topics, but two of the main ones were epistemology and purposes. The first exposed sharp differences in conceptions of science and scholarship, and the second went beyond the acceptance of the importance of values to ask what kind of values and which visions of purpose were most appropriate for the field. Just as most of the positions taken by critical theorists and subjectivists in educational administration reflect those positions as articulated in the social sciences and philosophy, so too do the criticisms made of the two views.

An unfortunate consequence of the debates in educational administration, as elsewhere, has been a tendency to simplify and lump together disparate views or to deal only with two extremes, ignoring other alternatives. Thus, textbooks in educational administration sometimes make misleading lists of dichotomous characteristics of, say positivism and phenomenology, in this case comparing an outdated positivism to which virtually no contemporary scholars subscribe with a phenomenology that bears little or no relation to the philosophy. A surprisingly common error is to lump functionalism and positivism together, possibly influenced by the simplistic classification scheme of Burrell and Morgan, which seems to have been swallowed whole by many of the less informed. Commenting on the relation of functionalism and positivism, Martindale, a student of sociological thought, wrote, "Sociological functionalism arose as a form of antipositivistic holism. . . ." He pointedly noted that Talcott Parsons made his advent in sociology "with a strong polemic against positivism and the subscription to a teleological conception of sociological subject matter," a phase of Parsons' orientation that he "never abandoned."[60] What did occur in sociology was that functionalism's heyday happened to coincide with the diffusion of more sophisticated, usually quantitative, research methods. However, functionalism was not especially compatible with such methods: puzzle over the measurement of a latent function! Nor were quantitative methods the same thing as philosophical positivism or logical empiricism. Still, functionalism and positivism were sometimes equated. However, this happens much more frequently today than it did when those perspectives were more popular and perhaps more carefully scrutinized. After all, they both make good targets for contemporary critics. My point is that they are quite different targets.

Misconceptions of the kind cited are spread during times of intellectual dissension when the contending parties create straw men and simplistic dichotomies. Unfortunately, they find fertile soil in fields like educational administration where many are not well schooled in philosophy and the social sciences and may have only a passing interest in some of the issues under discussion. In this connection, it is good to keep in mind that educational administration is a multipurpose field. This confers legitimacy on a wide variety of specializations and activities, but it also means that some individuals will be more than a little vulnerable to intellectual hucksterism in areas outside their specializations and interests. Put simply, partisan argumentation over the philosophic and scientific grounding of the field has sometimes confused, rather than enlightened, an audience that varied in its preparation to assess competing claims.

Despite the misconceptions and confusion, the underlying issues are real, and many counterarguments to the positions taken by critical theorists and subjectivists have been advanced. In educational administration, they emanate from a variety of sources and are usually directed to one or a few aspects of critical theory or subjectivism. Often, no general philosophical perspective is invoked in opposition to the two views, but when one is, it is likely to be a version of philosophical pragmatism. No current writers in educational administration call themselves positivists. Next are the criticisms of the criticisms.

Critical Theory: Criticisms

There is a substantial literature in philosophy and the social sciences that is critical of Marxism. Emphasized here, however, are points that apply to the critical theory version of neo-Marxism.[61] One is that the view is essentially a political ideology that exempts itself from the evaluative processes of inquiry. It pursues a pregiven political agenda rather than presenting ideas to be tested. Not surprisingly, Marxism is often compared to a religion since most of its internal debates over the years have concerned doctrinal issues, and praxis includes efforts to convert others. However, the chief debaters and proselytizers have been a relatively small number of intellectuals, while the working classes have remained essentially unmoved or opposed. In this connection, critical theorists have ignored the opportunities for upward mobility found in modern democracies. As a number of writers have pointed out, reproduction can be empirically assessed, and the results show that the effects of status origins are mediated by other factors, including education.[62]

The assumption by critical theorists of a monolithic ruling class that dominates all facets of society has been widely questioned. This assumption runs counter to the findings of studies in politics that show competition among multiple interests groups, the formation of temporary coalitions on particular issues, and that paint a generally more pluralistic picture of power and conflict than that found in critical theory.[63] An additional point is that, despite Marxian concerns about power elites, history teaches that nations with Marxist governments have had their own privileged classes along with oppressive state controls.

Another kind of issue arises with regard to the empirical studies of critical theorists. Here the issue is the interaction of the researcher's primary allegiance to an ideology of radical reform and the validity of the research. This is of special concern in ethnographic-type studies that are heavily dependent on observed perceptions and interpretations. Given the traditional Marxist distrust of empirical work, this issue has not been a central theme in the literature. However, it has been getting increasing attention in education, especially in connection with critical ethnography.[64]

Finally, critical theorists have been described as out of touch with and insensitive to the realities of practice in educational administration. Their preconceived notions of societal and educational change are utopian and scornful of mechanisms for reform currently available through democratically elected governing bodies. Their writings tend to be abstruse, full of Marxist jargon, and are often censorious and polemical, more in the style of debate than of civil discourse. Their depictions of school administrators as puppets of the ruling classes and schools as bastions of the status quo are exaggerated and unfair, betraying a lack of understanding of how both the conserving and critical activities of public school administrators and public schools are subject to norms for impartiality and equitability. Critical theorists may privilege their view of social reform as the one best way to social justice, but school administrators in their official capacities cannot endorse this or any partisan political program. As citizens, they are free to do as they wish, although it is hard to envision many of them advocating critical theory. Its combination of abstract ideology with uncompromising radical politics and portrayal of administrators as flunkies for regnant interests are likely to alienate most of them.

These criticisms represent a cross section from a variety of sources. They are criticisms that seem most relevant to the debates on critical theory in educational administration. However, it is good to keep in mind Held's comment that of all the attacks on critical theory, those of orthodox Marxists have been the harshest.[65]

Subjectivism: Criticisms

Various forms of subjectivism have been roundly criticized in philosophy and the social sciences.[66] However, the emphasis here will be on work pertinent to educational administration and, in particular, to

Greenfield's views. Since subjectivism emphasizes the unique experiences of the individual, it has difficulties with inter-subjectivity. Directly related is the charge of relativism. Stated somewhat differently by different writers, this charge has been leveled against Greenfield's subjectivism. Its substance is that in subjectivism no criteria are available to distinguish good ideas from bad ones.[67] Further, although one of the themes of Greenfield's writing has been an attack on the epistemology of others, he has not made his own explicit, a symptom of the difficulty of formulating a theory of knowledge once subjectivist assumptions have been made.

Greenfield's treatment of positivistic science has been described as an attack on a straw man. The version of science he sees is an outdated mechanistic one given to the discovery of ultimate truth. It bears little relation to the open, self-correcting processes of science that emphasize the tentativeness of all theory. Another aspect of Greenfield's writing on positivism concerns his objection to the separation of science and values that he sees in that view and in most educational administration scholarship. As noted earlier, Greenfield has not developed a systematic position on values, so Hodgkinson's values framework, which Greenfield cited approvingly, was critically discussed. Lakomski, however, took a different approach. She contended that Greenfield assumed the separation of values and facts as positivism does, thus separating values from relevant empirical content. She also applied the relativism argument to values stating that, if subjectivists are consistent, they have no basis on which to choose among competing values other than personal preference.[68]

Subjectivism is somewhat harder to put in context than critical theory, lacking as it does, the elaborate ideology and political program of that view. As articulated by Greenfield, subjectivism in educational administration has been, more than anything else, a critique of positivistic science and quantification. Beyond broad commitments to the individual, values, and a general humanism, a positive agenda that can be assessed and compared with others has yet to be formulated. It may be that Greenfield will be content if his criticisms nudge the field in the direction of those broad commitments. What remains to be done is the development of a deeper and more constructive conception of the kind of theorizing, empirical work and values that are in harmony with this general point of view and appropriate for educational administration. However, to the extent that such efforts are genuinely subjectivistic, they will have to deal with criticisms of the kind just discussed.

CHAPTER 2

Reconstructing the Future

WHERE does all this leave educational administration? Obviously, intellectual discourse and debate have their initial and strongest impact on scholarship and on university teaching. The attacks of neo-Marxists and subjectivists on social science and on what they perceive as dominant theoretical perspectives have created ferment in educational administration as in other fields. Often vigorously and even polemically expressed, their arguments have both shaken the intellectual tree and refocused scholarly discussion on such topics as values, justice, and individuality.

However, most of their views continue to be controversial because of the indiscriminate nature of their criticisms and the one-sidedness of their opinions. In a major review of theoretical trends in sociology, Alexander asserted that such one-sidedness has made it impossible to sustain the two broad lines of thought that have marked what he called the postfunctionalist phase in sociology. These lines of thought, which, respectively, include the two perspectives discussed, have lost their momentum and begun to decline, according to Alexander. He stated that "where even 10 years ago the air was filled with demands for radical and one-sided theoretical programs, in the contemporary period one can only hear calls for theorizing of an entirely different sort."[69] The latter he described as general theorizing that is synthetic rather than polemical.

Educational administration has in the past been greatly influenced by trends in fields like sociology. Thus, it is quite possible that changes there will contribute to the decline of critical theory and subjectivist thinking in educational administration. However, there are some important differences. In sociology, Marxist macrotheory and microtheories that emphasized the individual became very strong, even dominant, during the recent past. In educational administration, such perspectives, represented by critical theory and subjectivism, have been more marginal. Furthermore, educational administration, in common with other applied fields, has weaker theoretical and research traditions than sociology. So it is unclear whether these critical views have yet to peak in educational administration or are already waning. It is also possible that one of the two views or aspects of them will have greater staying power or will develop by combining with another strand of thought as, for example, in neo-Marxian feminist studies.

However, just as the spirit of the times in the 1960s and 1970s promoted the spread of these critical views, the 1980s and probably the 1990s will be less hospitable. The reformist and individualistic urges of the earlier period were replaced by more conservative ones in the 1980s. In addition, many contemporary problems such as urban disintegration, the environment, the AIDS epidemic, abortion, drug addiction, and conflict rooted in cultural and religious differences do not fit the ideological patterns and political alignments of the past. Of major negative significance for all forms of Marxism has been the collapse of many governments that had espoused Marxist ideas as official doctrine. These governments were brought down by popular demand from all segments of their citizenry, including the working classes, in a kind of people's revolution that was not what Marx had envisioned. The clear point was that when Marxists had opportunities to govern, their programs of state socialism did not work very well. They fared far worse on both the economic and human rights fronts than the liberal democratic governments that Marxist scholars so frequently castigate.

Less clear-cut is the apparent diminution of the extreme individualism that spawned the so-called "me" generation. Now preoccupied with their jobs and family responsibilities, the members of this cohort seem to have largely replaced the egocentric radicalism of their youth with a more moderate and more community-oriented outlook.

It would seem that all of these forces will work against critical theory and subjectivism just as the equivalent forces of an earlier period worked in their behalf. However, universities are sheltered places, especially in democratic nations, and they reflect what many academics aptly call the real world, in unpredictable ways.

ADVOCACY, CONFUSION, INVIGORATION

Writing a dozen years ago, Griffiths titled an article "Intellectual Turmoil in Educational Administration."[70] Whatever the fates of critical theory and subjectivism, it appears that there is still a considerable amount of confusion in the field, if not turmoil. At least some of the confusion can probably be attributed to the abrasiveness of much of the discourse over the directions and purposes of thought and research in educational administration. As suggested earlier, advocacy taken to extremes can result in the presentation of overly simplified, often dichotomous alternatives, not to mention a kind of we-them mentality.

Used to having ideas advanced tentatively, many professors of educational administration were uncertain about how to assess the sweeping assertions made by critical theorists and by Greenfield, especially in light of the critics' claim that the evaluative processes of science were flawed and irrelevant. Although both the critical theory version of neo-Marxism and subjectivism had been standard fare in philosophy and sociology for a very long time, they were new to those in educational administration who were unfamiliar with those fields. One or another of these views was adopted by those to whom they appealed, including some who were uncomfortable with the social science emphasis in educational administration and others who embraced that emphasis with the expectation that it would be a panacea.

Today, many seem chary of social science, distrust both critical theory and subjectivism, and are tired of the "intellectual turmoil," which, in any case, they see as having little direct impact on what happens in schools. Both turmoil and confusion can spawn doubt, hesitation, and a certain lack of confidence. What is called for is an invigoration of the professorial culture in educational administration. I believe three things are especially important.

The first is the diffusion of a conception of inquiry that sees science for what it is, a human activity that is highly dependent on individual creativity and interpretation, that has its limits, and that has had its failures as well as its successes—a science that is open to all sorts of ideas but strives to be self-critical using practical standards of verification devised and maintained within the various disciplinary communities. Discussions on science in the educational administration disciplinary community need to be more constructive than they have been in recent years. The aim, after all, should be enhanced understanding of educational institutions and their administration.

The second is more explicit attention to values and valuation. This should encompass both ideal possibilities and the situationally-given value judgments required daily of administrators. Most of the recent discussion of values in educational administration has deplored their deemphasis but has been short on what values should be emphasized and why.

The third is a more thoughtful exploration of the practice of educational administration. Practice has its empirical side, dealing with what administrators believe and how they behave. It also can be considered in terms of what it could become at its best. Of great importance here is the notion of informed or thoughtful practice, that is, praxis. While sundry politicians and commissions have not hesitated to assess the practice of educational administration, usually negatively, the topic has not been at the forefront of scholarship in educational administration. Theories of practice are sorely lacking.

Next, each of these three areas is considered. Obviously, my selection of the areas and what I have to say about them reflect my perceptions of the state of the field and my opinions about the philosophic and scientific grounding of scholarship and practice in educational administration. Despite some reservations and some differences, my views are closer to philosophical pragmatism than to other philosophical positions.[71] I like its skepticism about formal philosophic systems; its rejection of unexamined creeds and absolutes; its openness to ideas as hypotheses to be examined and tried out; its focus on inquiry and reflection as human activities that can often go wrong but can lead to warranted assertibility; its blending of the normative and descriptive; its emphasis on the individual and community in a context of freedom, democracy, and growth; and, finally, its optimism. Even the title of this chapter, "Reconstructing the Future," alludes to the Deweyan concept of the deliberate, reflective reconstruction of experience that creates a fuller, richer experience.

Having given fair warning about my personal preferences, I want to make clear that there are a number of philosophies that could help educational administration construct a desirable future.[72] However, I believe that philosophical pragmatism offers more advantages and has far fewer Achilles' heels than its competitors, patently so in the cases of neo-Marxism, subjectivism, and positivism.

INQUIRY

It would be easy to argue that educational administration requires a new kind of inquiry or science. Easy and perhaps appealing to those who like new things, but not honest. Educational administration needs a conception of science that might be novel to some, or even many, scholars but is not new, any more than the issues raised by subjectivists, neo-Marxist critical theorists, or those engaged in the qualitative-quantitative debates are new.

The polemical side of the subjectivists' and critical theorists' attacks have only muddied the waters. Greenfield's robot-like social scientists and administrators, heartless, without compassion, lacking in high purpose, and thoroughly deficient as human beings and the critical theorists' picture of them as lackeys doing the bidding of the ruling classes are mere rhetorical stereotypes sustained by ideology, not evidence. They go hand in hand with the self-centered and oddly similar portraits of epistemological debate each of the two positions paints: that is, of itself locked in combat with an extreme scientistic positivism, a portrait that ignores every reasonable epistemological position in favor of a fight with a straw man.

To be taken more seriously are charges that the social sciences and scientific methods don't work or are irrelevant and should be replaced by something else such as dialectical analysis, phenomenological methods, or hermeneutics. It is my impression that the expectations of the social sciences held in educational administration in the late 1950s and 1960s were unrealistically high. Many believed that if a better understanding of schools and their contexts could be attained, improvements in education would follow. The first happened, but nothing could guarantee the second. Ironically, the social sciences themselves examine the complex forces and processes that make it so difficult to use knowledge effectively to solve social problems and bring about social change. Social decisions are typically grounded in self-interested, often narrow or even irrational beliefs and ideologies. Simple certainties are much more comfortable than theories and probabilities. The thirty-second analysis with simple solution is not really a creature of the television age. Its forebears and its kin are legion, as social science makes clear.

Even though the concepts and theories of social science can furnish new and more adequate ways of seeing situations and can even help in making rough predictions about desired courses of action, there are no sure things and no panaceas.

Science by People

Science just does not deal with certainties; it is not a search for final truths. What is really distinctive about it is the attitude it fosters and the procedures it cultivates. Examples are curiosity about how things work, the creation of tentative explanations or theories, and commitment to critical and public assessment of them. The norms of science are not carved in stone, but are developed and maintained by people. Most of these norms are geared to skeptical open-mindedness, impersonal criteria of evaluation, and the communication of results.[73] There are, of course, differences in emphasis by specialty, with more stringent standards in fields where prediction and replication are less ambiguous.

In educational administration, the norms, as I see them, are quite open and inclusive. This is reinforced by the multipurpose character of the field and the diversity of its publication outlets that range from those that stress empirical studies or theoretical essays to those that focus mainly on current issues or timely topics in education or dispense tips on practice. The field's relatively weak research culture is reflected in the uneven quality of publications in the more scholarly journals. Worst cases include the overkill of tightly designed quantitative studies on trivial problems and feeling pieces relating personal experiences and reactions in a usually gripping school situation.

Despite all this, I believe that overall, scientific norms have been applied quite reasonably in educational administration. The appliers, of course, have been the field's community of scholars: editorial evaluators, reviewers, and anyone who has cited and commented on another's work. They appear to operationalize scientific norms by attending to such issues as the importance of the problem examined; the logic, clarity, and originality of the theoretical reasoning; and the care taken in designing the study and its methods. While everyone has horror stories to tell about their experiences with editors and reviewers, those who have such responsibilities seem, on the whole, to be committed to fairness and quality. It is far-fetched to claim, as is occasionally done, that there is some kind of insiders' club devoted to one kind of thinking and research that excludes everything else. My experience as an editorial board member and reader has been quite the opposite. New ideas, original thinking, something off the beaten path, is usually eagerly welcomed, provided that it is clearly communicated. Good work of this kind is customarily very well received in the field. For instance, Wolcott's ethnographic study of an elementary principal, published well before the subjectivist critique in educational administration, was highly praised when it appeared and is still cited approvingly. This study was anything but an example of the "blitzkrieg ethnography" that was later criticized. It involved field observations over an extended period, was a model of thick description, and devoted considerable space to issues of bias and method.[74] Similarly, Willis' study, discussed earlier, has been quite widely applauded because of its empathetic depiction of its protagonists, working class boys called "the lads," and its careful examination of their plight.[75] The reception accorded these studies suggests two things: the openness of the field to various methods and perspectives and the imposition of standards of quality. These were especially good studies of their types.

I use them to illustrate a point: Scientific norms are constructed by various scientific communities and interpreted by them to make judgments about theory and research. These judgments take into account the purposes and type of the research and recognize that different methods have different strengths and weaknesses and that some kinds of subject matter are difficult to pin down very compellingly. Actually, neither of these two critically acclaimed studies pin very much down very compellingly. Both are ethnographic, one more or less traditional cultural anthropology, the other neo-Marxist in orientation. Yet both were characterized by careful and, extended field observations; specific attention to the problems of bias and where recognized, its explication; and richly textured conceptual exposition. To give just one example of the latter, Willis' discussion of how the shared, ego-protecting, class-based norms adopted by the lads diminished the likelihood of upward mobility for them sheds light on the nature of cultural conflict in a way that is full of implications for education and for the societal problem of blocked life chances.

Of course, one should not go overboard concerning these studies; both had their share of shortcomings. After all, the same scientific attitudes that exult in careful empirical work and insightful theorizing also foster a continuing skepticism and a sensitivity to limitations and weaknesses. My intention was to suggest, in a general way, how scientific norms actually operate in a field like educational administration. The realities of social science are anything but lock step and dehumanized. Science is fundamentally a very human activity. It requires judgment and sometimes compromises with the standards for ideal science that have evolved in scholarly communities. For instance, exact replication is desirable, but in nonexperimental social science, its stand-in is detailed description of what one did as an investigator so that someone else could use similar procedures in another setting. In spite of such compromises and the differences found in the various specializations, most scholars appear to subscribe to the kind of norms for combined skepticism and open-mindedness, public communication, and impersonal evaluation cited earlier.

Some Philosophical Concerns

The kind of practical empiricism that is reflected in scientific norms has served inquiry admirably and has lessons for some armchair philosophers as well. For instance, the theory-ladenness of observations is not a major problem for scientists who recognize that eventually some of the theories that guide observations will be seen to work better than others, nor is the matter of generalizations or laws in science, including social science. Theorizing conventionally employs the language of causality. How something works is unconditionally specified by hypothesizing the relationships among concepts. The logic and plausibility of this specification figure in the evaluation of a theory. However, it is understood in science that generalizations should also be assessed in evidential terms, which lead to sometimes quite rough judgments of probability. The term *law,* when used, simply refers to a generalization of extraordinarily high probability. The main point is that nothing is final or certain. Plausibility and probability within a self-corrective framework are science's best outcomes.

The presented conception of science is both practical and philosophically sound. It is not wedded to philosophical realism or to a naive empiricism. Scientific norms evolve as hypotheses themselves, and science needs no outside foundation or ultimate justification.[76] Put simply, science is a set of attitudes and processes that have worked far better than any of the broad alternatives such as authority, faith, or intuition. Its open and self-critical nature and its emphasis on the creation and free expression of ideas and their public communication and assessment foster values that reject dogmatism and embrace originality, freedom, and skepticism. Such a conception of science encourages the use of multiple perspectives and methods but exempts none of them from critical scrutiny and evaluation.

Claims and Possibilities

This brings us to a consideration of the claims made for dialectical analysis, phenomenological methods, and hermeneutics. I see all three as useful conceptual orientations and procedures. None of them is inconsistent with science. Problems arise, however, when outlandish claims are made: namely, that one or another of these methods is the way to understanding and all others should be forsaken in its favor. A problem of another kind is that these methods are rarely set forth so that they can be clearly understood, a situation exacerbated by writers who state or imply that this cannot be done easily because of the complexity or rigor involved. The mystification that such writers foster begins to fade with the realization that all three methods are simply forms of reasoning, introspective to be sure, but communicated via logical discourse.

Grounded in Hegel's familiar thesis-antithesis-synthesis, dialectical analysis has been used by Marxists in various ways. Marx employed it to comprehend historical necessity and the revolutionary change of capitalism (thesis) into its antithesis, the proletarian dictatorship, and finally to synthesis, an ideal communist society. This is, of course, a flawed and outdated view of history, even to most Marxists. More recent neo-Marxian usages tend either to equate dialectical analysis with any argument made within a Marxist framework or to elaborate particular points related to the general notion of dialectical change, for example, the concept of contradiction. The former approach has been much more in evidence than the latter.[77] As noted earlier, phenomenological methods, as elaborated by Husserl, required a bracketing of presuppositions that allowed the mind to experience, through a kind of directed intuition, the essence of the concept under study.[78] Hermeneutics was also discussed previously. Here it is good to emphasize that, like phenomenological methods, hermeneutics in its purer forms uses particular procedures to guide the interpretive processes.[79] When hermeneutics or phenomenological methods are used to mean ordinary reflection or interpretation, they lose much of their special flavor. The looser rendering of them is very common today in the social sciences and education. This rendering is, of course, correct in the sense that all of these methods are, in the end, forms of human reflection.

Each is quite useful. The dialectic reminds us of the limitations of linear and incremental thinking. It fits concepts such as threshold effect and directs attention to the phenomena of opposition, conflict, and dramatic change. However, it is essentially a starting point and guide for the development of ideas. It offers little useful explanation about the forces it emphasizes. The phenomenological precept, "Back to the things themselves," is more than a statement of disagreement with Kant. It refers to the intuitively given essence of a thing (read concept) that remains when all presuppositions, prior judgments, and dogmas have been removed. This is an intriguing regimen; eliminating the extraneous to expose the pith has been a longstanding intellectual ideal. I have suggested elsewhere that phenomenologically oriented scholars in educational administration might study this method and attempt the phenomenological analysis of relevant concepts. In this connection, it seems unreasonable to expect that two phenomenologists examining the same concept would come up with the same results. In any case, that is an empirical matter and not critical if the chief aim is insight. Hermeneutics offers a set of important and useful processes for the exploration of the meaning of texts. Beyond that, it is vaguer than the other two methods and is often used simply to refer to subjective interpretation in its broadest sense. In this guise, jargonish concepts like "the hermeneutic imagination" are often favored, and what Rorty called the "edifying qualities of hermeneutics" are stressed rather than its epistemological ones.[80]

Still, it is only when someone paints one of these methods (or any method) as the royal road to understanding that problems arise. More likely these days, however, is to compare one or another of these approaches with a rigid positivism or other easy target, as was done in a recent article in educational administration that offered some useful comments about leadership but made a philosophically naive case for hermeneutics, as compared with a kind of simple-minded empiricism.[81] The misleading dichotomy it emphasized stands in sharp contrast to the more sophisticated view of hermeneuticists such as the Dilthey scholar H. P. Rickman. He argued that hermeneutics "is not intended as an exclusive alternative to the scientific approach but as a supplement to it." Noting that hermeneutics and science share "common procedures, such as classification and deduction," and that "interpretation depends on factual evidence and scientific objectivity depends on reliable communication," Rickman summarized his view of successful social science research as a combination of "scientific study of facts with methodical interpretation of meaning."[82]

Here, hermeneutics takes its place with science to abet the interpretation of human communication. Emphasized are the creative sides of science: making sense of results and devising theory. Whatever we call this aspect of science, it is as essential as its critical, verificational side. If dialectical or subjectivistically oriented methods can contribute something constructive, so much the better. This, after all, is where they belong, that is, as contributors to inquiry where they can do so, not as exclusive or privileged procedures.[83]

A problem for subjectivism and neo-Marxism, which Collins pointed out in connection with sociology, is that these views gained prominence by attacking positivistic science and are "emotionally committed to the polemic, especially when it has political overtones or when it is couched in the rhetoric of the human and the living versus the dead hands of alienated science." At some point, Collins contended, the shouting about directions should stop, and the critics should show they can produce something more impressive than what they attacked.[84] However, neither neo-Marxism nor subjectivism gave priority to the development of distinctive programs of empirical research. Indeed, well-received research done by scholars of either persuasion is not likely to abandon scientific standards. Despite occasional rhetorical flourishes, it usually adheres to them. I praised the Willis study because it was good field research; I saw its neo-Marxist bias, which the author was explicit about, as a limitation and a weakness. In any case, one must wonder with Collins at what point polemics will end and constructive work in line with the critics' views of science will begin.

Science as It Is

Perhaps more important in educational administration than whether the critics can go beyond criticism and make much of a substantive contribution to understanding educational institutions is the matter of the regeneration of enthusiasm for serious empirical scholarship in the field after fifteen years of heated attacks on the legitimacy and value of scientific inquiry.

It is important that science be seen for the many things it is: a challenge to wit and ingenuity, an adventure in the creation, testing, and modification of ideas, an exercise in skepticism and the rigors of public evaluation, a way of sharing curiosity and puzzle-solving experiences with students and colleagues, and an opportunity to communicate new understandings that could be put to use by others. I admit to a tendency to stress the creative, hypothesis-constructing side of science out of personal interest but make no mistake about the vitality and efficacy of the critical or verificational side of science. Judgments about the logic and coherence of theory and the empirical credibility of observations are at the heart of inquiry. The practical empiricism of science, as opposed to a naive or literal empiricism, is alive and well. If it weren't, as Collins put it for sociology, we would be "back in the Middle Ages taking orders from philosophical dogmatists."[85]

The norms of science, human creations and hypotheses that they are, work. After all, airplanes fly, hearts can be transplanted, and key norms of school teacher and administrator groups are highly predictable. Science and its underlying norms are durable because they evolved in a trial and error fashion. What we've got might well be improved but it is open, public, and the product of experience and experiment in its broadest sense. So while science and its norms are made by people, they are not a matter of whim. That is why inquiry tailored to suit an ideology, a particular culture, or a special-interest group won't work. That there is plenty of bias, dogma, closed-mindedness, and self-interest in the human condition is comprehended in the character of scientific norms, which are geared to minimizing such qualities and maximizing their opposites. Science as it is, emerges as epistemologically sound and as an engaging, exciting, and valuable human activity. Understanding this is a first step toward the renewal of enthusiasm for inquiry in educational administration.

VALUES

There is virtually universal agreement that values play a key role in administration.[86] But the agreement ends at that point, and there is only a limited amount of relevant scholarship. That values should be acknowledged everywhere to be crucial in educational administration, yet not be a major focus of scholarly attention, seems an anomaly. However, there are many reasons for this state of affairs, which is not unique to educational administration but is found as well in comparable fields like business and public administration.

The influence of logical positivism has been exaggerated. Its emphasis on the linguistic distinction between is and ought statements was, of course, correct, but its separation of science and values was not. Whatever the impact of this philosophical view, other factors seemed more important. One was educational administration's orientation to specific value issues rather than to broader philosophic treatments of values. Values concerns in the field were absorbed in current issues, many of them connected with specific equity questions, not more abstract axiological ones, which some professors felt unprepared to discuss in philosophic terms in any case. Another was that the energies of many of the best scholars in the field were devoted to empirical studies, work that was facilitated by the array of concepts, theories, and methodologies that became available as a result of educational administration's turn toward the social sciences. A third was the reluctance of scholars to seem to impose their values on others, especially in a society committed to democratic theory and the control of education by the public, not by experts. Finally, the development of systematic approaches to values was a daunting undertaking with few guidelines and the promise of outcomes that were likely to be controversial. Furthermore, positions on ethics and values in philosophy such as hedonism, Plato's Idea of the Good, Kant's categorical imperative, utilitarianism, and various kinds of transcendentalism seemed irrelevant and out of touch with the realities of administrative life. And the same can be said for the offerings of critical theorists and subjectivists in educational administration, although both served useful purposes by insisting on the importance of values.

Some Moral Choices

Moral choices are made daily by administrators. Educational administration requires approaches to values that can usefully inform those choices. I will present one such approach, a theory of valuation that takes the context of judgments about values in administration into account. It recognizes that moral choice does not really occur when the selection is between a clear good and a clear evil. That kind of decision is as easy to make as it is rare. Most administrative problems are in the grayer areas, choices between competing goods or the lesser of evils. Many of these problems arise situationally and are not related to administrators' deliberate plans to advance their organizations in ways that enhance certain values.

Let us take as an example a teacher with a drinking problem. General outcomes that are desirable are not difficult to discern: The welfare of the teacher and the welfare of the students are obvious ones. Beyond that, there is a host of questions. Among them are the likelihood that the teacher will be able to cope successfully with the problem, whether there are strategies for communicating with the teacher in ways that will help rather than make matters worse, and how to determine the point at which the students' education begins to suffer enough to justify intervention. Notice that the valued outcomes in this case are quite clear. The difficult part is making predictive judgments about the consequences of courses of action or of inaction.

As a second example, suppose that, after some study and consultation, a school administrator decides to embark on a program of curricular change. This case differs from the first in that it is not thrust upon the administrator but is deliberately initiated to implement a vision of school improvement.[87] In common with the first case, however, numerous predictive judgments would be required. Beyond the obvious question of whether the change will lead to the hoped for improvements in student learning, they would deal with such matters as the politics of adoption and opposition both in the organization and the community, the likelihood of various responses and reactions from different individuals and groups, and the feasibility and efficacy of logistical and technical approaches to implementation. Careful planning would probably also include attempts to anticipate and head off unintended consequences.

The point of all this is that judgments of value and judgments of fact are intertwined and interdependent in administrative life. Judgments about the probability of various courses of action leading to particular results are necessary if informed moral choices are to be made. Obviously, such judgments will be tricky and uncertain. In effect, they will be hypotheses, but like hypotheses in science, they will benefit if they are theoretically informed. Put differently, social science concepts and theories, far from being something that should be separated from valuation as logical positivism suggested, are essential to intelligent moral action. I would give high priority to the place of science in valuation. First, the process itself is classic Deweyan reflective methods, the same kind of activity that characterizes scientific inquiry. Second, as already suggested, the content of social science is relevant to the admittedly fallible predictions that thoughtful moral choice entails. Third, my sense of things is that most school administrators and educators are committed to helping students learn and grow as human beings. Many of them appear to be quite altruistic. However, good intentions, even a good heart, are not enough in administration. Visions of what an educational organization at its best can become are capable of inspiring and directing belief and action but, by themselves, guarantee nothing. The main problem is negotiating the pitfalls and complexities of modern organizational and social life to get to something better. In this, the methods and theories of social inquiry wedded to a morally sensitive vision of human possibilities offer the best hope of concrete progress. And note that this view of valuation, like the epistemological position presented earlier, is inclusive and open, rather than stressing a pregiven set of absolute values.

Some Practical Problems

Two additional problems merit consideration. One is common to all administration; the other is of special concern in educational administration. The first is the matter of compromise and the half a loaf issue. Since administration involves conflict and the coordination of varied interests, compromise is a frequent strategy. In mediating conflict among individuals and groups in the organization, it is often possible to serve desirable ends since such ends come with built-in rationales and the administrator commonly has the authority or the influence to effect a resolution. Here, compromise might well be ignored in the light of a clearly better alternative or else might involve giving the losers something connected with a side issue. More significant in values terms is the "half a loaf is better than none" compromise. In such a case the administrator concludes that a valued objective can be only partially attained and settles for less. This is an area connected with values where little is known. We need to understand better what influences the decision to disengage, the differences between realistic disengagement and the failure of courage, and factors that accompany drastic disengagement such as resigning a position because of a clash of values. In any case, the interplay of principle, feasibility, and survival in administration is an intriguing puzzle having special relevance to values and valuation.

The second area is important in public administration and especially in educational administration. The problem here is the extent to which school administrators and other school personnel should try to impose their viewpoints and the extent to which they should, in a society committed to democracy, attempt to follow the views of the majority of the citizens of the community. There are, of course, stock answers that make a lot of sense: that it is up to school administrators to educate the public and build support for programs aimed at the improvement of schooling and that school officials are responsible to their boards of education, which represent the community and reflect its views in their policy decisions. I raise the question because most discussions of values fail to place administrators in this kind of context. Actions are idealized by our hopes for better schools, a better society, and a better world. The assumption is made that, armed with the right values and a little charisma, school administrators will make good things happen. Perhaps so. I have already suggested that most of them are good-hearted. The issue here, however, is the responsibility of public officials to the public, especially when those public officials are also defined as "experts" or professionals.

Having initially framed the problem in terms of majority values, it is necessary to consider the matter of minority values. While majority rule is a democratic precept, a distinctive ideal of American democracy has been its concern with the rights of the minority and of dissenters of all kinds. This ideal has evolved substantially since it was enshrined in the Bill of Rights, but the successes in recent decades of racial and ethnic minorities and feminists attest to its continuing vitality. While these groups pursue their agendas with vigor and considerable sophistication, others on the outside, lacking the benefit of organized effort, have remained inarticulate. However, at least in American society, where victimization is becoming a growth industry and support groups the social clubs of the day, some who were previously silent are now being heard. In any case, most school administrators face a public that is heterogeneous in both make-up and viewpoint. Here, a challenge is to provide mechanisms for the school's many constituencies, not just the articulate and the powerful, to give expression to their values.

At the same time, it is one thing to seek opinions that reflect underlying values and another to assess them. Forums that lack procedures for critical assessment are likely to be self-defeating. However much we may respect the rights of everyone to an opinion and even solicit opinions on public issues, the simple truth is that, from a philosophic perspective, the values of some individuals and collectivities fare better than others. In these terms, some cultures are better than others. In this connection, it is good to keep in mind that cultures are frequently insular and intolerant of dissent and of outsiders; they commonly promote conformity and stifle attempts at self-criticism. This is the darker side of culture that clashes with the proposition that moral choices should be treated as hypotheses and critically assessed.

The first part of this analysis dealt essentially with the process of valuation itself, the weighing of alternative moral choices and the evaluation of their probable consequences. The present discussion of how to balance the views of school personnel and the public now leads to a further point of some consequence. It is the matter of institutionalizing procedures for the expression and assessment of value positions, a significant concern for public organizations like schools, although it is a concern that is often neglected.

I will consider institutionalization of this kind in the section to follow on praxis, so I will deal with it only briefly here. The main point is that, on issues of importance to the public or segments of it, routine and regular means should be available for airing and assessing views on controversial issues. The issues could be quite specific, such as whether to close an elementary school building. Here, values that emphasized community, comfort, and familiarity might clash with values stressing cost-effectiveness and greater availability of space and instructional resources. Or the issue could be more general, as in the consideration of alternative school futures.

Such opportunities for expression are not uncommon in education. However, they are often polite formalities, the chance to have one's say. While that chance should not be minimized, the process can be ritualistic. A formidable difficulty is that people typically take preestablished positions rather than treating proposals as hypotheses to be examined. Of course, such examination often results in the early demise of some proposals, but in such cases reasons can be cited. A critical analysis that explores probable consequences and their desirability means that a proposal is taken both seriously and skeptically. Treating all proposals in this fashion, even those of the chief administrator, also speaks to the problem raised earlier about administrator versus community values. Furthermore, a venting of what might go wrong if a course of action is adopted can result in coordinated plans to deal with anticipated negative consequences that might accompany an otherwise desirable decision.

The general approach to values set forth emphasizes concrete moral choices and their consequences in social contexts and suggests practical reflective methods for selecting among alternatives. This kind of approach is generally considered strong on method, but weak on the prior specification of desired ends. The other side of the coin is that, while a value system that goes very far in specifying such ends is likely to state a variety of obviously good ones, its basic flaw will be its inability to resolve satisfactorily the problem of competing desired ends. If there is any overriding desirable end in the position presented, it is probably human growth as represented by the reconstruction and enrichment of experience made possible by reflective and critical methods.[88]

In exploring the topic of values, I have tried to present a constructive and, I hope, realistic position. I also examined several issues that illustrate the array and complexity of value questions in the field. They go well beyond the pseudo-issue of whether values should have a recognized place in scholarship in educational administration and foreshadow an agenda for future inquiry. I turn now to the topic of practice. However, the discussion of values just completed is full of implications for practice, and that on practice should elucidate some remaining questions on values. The two are truly intertwined, for as Dewey reminds us "Morals has to do with all activity into which alternative possibilities enter."[89]

PRAXIS

The term *praxis* is used here in the sense of informed or thoughtful practice. This reflects the conception of administrative action presented, although I use the term somewhat reluctantly because it sounds more pretentious than practice.

As is known from a number of studies, the daily work of school administration consists of a stream of fast-paced activities and interactions. These activities and interactions are typically brief and varied. Most of them are unscheduled, although school superintendents and, to a lesser extent, school principals spend a fair amount of time in scheduled meetings. These studies show administrator preferences for face-to-face verbal communication; a great deal of the work is accomplished by talking with others, usually in person, but also by telephone. The administrators are drawn to live action, giving immediate attention to crises or to problems that can be quickly resolved. Self-initiated changes to more pressing or speedily handled activities combine with other interruptions to fragment the work day.[90]

Despite the intensity of activity and the persistent complaints and conflict they face, most administrators like their jobs and offset stress (which seems to be a variable rather than a constant phenomenon among school officials) through a variety of devices, including exercise and outside interests. They lighten burdensome problems through humor, especially in peer interactions. Both district-level and building-level school executives are engaged in tasks that serve a wide variety of purposes. Among the most time-consuming are organizational maintenance and internal and external interpersonal relationships; however, the facilitation and improvement of instruction also receive a good deal of attention, although administrators usually cite them as activities they want to devote more time to. Educational administrators are sensitive to the vulnerability of their public organizations and give high priority to protecting them. They commonly act decisively to head off or dampen perceived threats.[91]

Deciding

Most studies of school administrators are simply not designed to provide insights into the thought processes of these executives. However, the picture of hectic activity that emerges from the studies of the allocation of time and attention does not suggest strong commitments to reflective decision making or the thoughtful selection of a preferred moral choice from among competing alternatives as a chief or even secondary aspect of administrator activity.

However, other studies show the importance of strategy and tactics to administrators, and a few inquiries in educational administration have directly examined decision processes with interesting results. One of the earliest of these studies, the "in-basket" research of the 1960s, indicated that working hard at planning ahead was associated with the measures of success employed in that inquiry. A recent investigation of expert versus typical principals showed that, especially for less routine or unstructured problems, the decisions of the experts exhibited more of the following characteristics: detailed prior planning, information collection, careful thinking, consultation, flexibility, range of goals, ability to connect shorter range goals to broader principles, coherence across solution components, and self-confidence.[92] Such studies suggest the utility of more reflective processes and informed choice.

There have not been very many inquiries of this kind. Moreover, criticism of rational decision making has been a popular pastime in the social sciences spurred by organized anarchy and garbage can theorists and by those who associate such decision making with a mechanistic and positivistic science (reminding us of Greenfield's all too inhuman administrators!). As an aside, it might be noted that, in an odd quirk of language, writing on *reflective* as opposed to *rational* decision making seems not to have been as attractive a target. What critics of rational decision making appear to have missed is the normative thrust of that work. No one claims that decisions are, in fact, made rationally. Many are irrational and some are just lucky. The claim is that rational processes for decision making can be worked out and can be employed by those who choose to do so. The main empirical supposition is that such decisions will be more likely to work than other kinds.[93]

While claims for the advantages of rational decision making seem reasonable and tend to be supported by studies of the kind cited, it is clear that most administrators just do not devote a lot of time and energy to reflective analysis. This is not surprising given the incessant demands of the work, the reactive nature of much of it, the complexities of organizational life, the frequency of decisions that are close calls in the sense that a good case can be made for each alternative, the intellectual effort required by the thoughtful scanning and evaluation of courses of action and their probable consequences. In addition, some administrators rightly recognize the fallibility of reflective methods and fear the paralysis of overanalysis. Finally, planning may be associated with routines and reports to be avoided or ritualized as seems to have happened so often in cases where strategic planning has been adopted.

It is also possible that administrators are more deliberate in their actions than appears on the surface. For instance, they may make judgments of relative importance and reserve more extensive analysis for more significant problems. Another possibility is that what appear to be snap judgments in administration are actually grounded in a process of pattern recognition. This was proposed by Herbert Simon based on expert-novice research done with such varied groups as chess players, physicians, and business administrators. The experts were able to solve problems quickly, without being able to report just how they did it. What was done by the novices with much conscious and explicit analysis was done rapidly with the appearance of intuition by the experts. Simon's hypothesis of pattern recognition drew on the analogy of language: experts have learned over time to recognize a very large number of patterns comparable to the vocabulary of one's natural language. Just as word recognition brings with it meaning and other associations, pattern recognition brings information about its significance, dangers, and utilities. Simon contended that when problems are more than trivial, "The recognition processes have to be organized in a coherent way and they must be supplied with reasoning capabilities that allow inferences to be drawn . . . and chunks of information to be combined." He suggested that conscious deliberation and expert intuition of patterns are complementary components of effective decisions. Given the complexity of all this, one can only agree with Simon's admonition that "a vast research and development task of extracting and cataloging the knowledge and cues used by the experts in different kinds of managerial tasks lies ahead."[94] In educational administration, such research represents an exciting prospect that has barely gotten started.

Clark has argued that one of the problems with most traditional theories is that they differ "too markedly from the logic-in-use in organizations."[95] Along these lines, one can hope that qualitative studies will reflect the current logic-in-use better than some other forms of research, but a more fundamental question that arises from Simon's analysis is that of the importance of direct inquiry into "logic-in-use" itself. While Clark's use of the term communicates quite well as "how sense is made of things," there are obvious needs for definition and differentiation. Simon's pattern recognition hypothesis has one kind of focus; the more philosophical concern with moral choice has another;

and an emphasis on administrator beliefs, norms, assumptions, and language has still another. Respectively, psychological, philosophical, and sociological in orientation, these approaches represent overlapping but distinct scholarly thrusts, none of which is well developed in educational administration. The last of the three, the sociological, has had the most attention. We know quite a lot about the organizational context of practice, but its consequences for decision making are less clear. How administrators decide on one course of action rather than another is not very well understood.

Deliberation

Conscious, explicit choice requires deliberation. Indeed, to deliberate about the proper handling of an administrative problem is itself a choice. Setting aside all administrative decisions that are routine, trivial, or so clear-cut that assessment is unnecessary leaves a substantial number of choice situations that require deliberative attention. Deliberation itself is no guarantee of wise choice. Reasonable choice is a function of reflective deliberation that concerns itself with both short- and long-range consequences and with desirable rather than merely desired courses of action.[96] This kind of decision making, which is the very essence of praxis or thoughtful practice, was described when valuation was considered. Its emphasis on reflective methods, the treatment of alternative choices as hypotheses, and its use of social science concepts and theories are of particular value to practitioners in numerous ways. For instance, it helps administrators to see and reconstruct experience in diverse and richer forms. It reduces unintended consequences, or as Dewey put it, "An act tried out in imagination is not final or fatal. It is retrievable."[97] It frames problems and their solutions as subject matter for critical analysis, not as an administrator's or a faction's pregiven conclusion (the infamous solution looking for a problem). It reduces the likelihood of overly abstract decision making through its focus on particular courses of action and their probable consequences in concrete, locally contingent situations. And it is likely to provide a chosen alternative that is easy for an administrator to defend since it will have survived critical assessment, and potential side effects will already have been canvassed.

The kind of creative pursuit of problem solving depicted here is thoroughly scientific, yet anything but mechanical or lacking an emotional component. The reflective, scientific temper in administration fosters executive openness and an active engagement with ideas as their meaning and consequences are imaginatively scanned, played out, checked, and revised. The administrative life that results is presumably more robust, productive, and emotionally satisfying than one that is more passive. The Deweyan view of reflective methods aims at their internalization as habit. The idea is that they should eventually represent a natural, almost automatic response on the part of the individual. Intellect is not separated from impulse, desire, and passion. The false separation of intellect and emotion is seen as a moral tragedy that makes science seem cold and calculating and cuts off generous and sympathetic impulse and emotion from its best hope of clarification and realization. Character is described as a working interaction of habits, but even a good character cannot guarantee good results. Reflective methods can help to make that connection and can also be brought to bear in revising and readjusting habits.[98] This kind of self-aware and self-critical emphasis suggests G. H. Mead's concept of reflexiveness and, of course, the Socratic dictum to "know thyself," which is standard advice dispensed in administrator preparation programs. In the context of the present discussion, self-knowledge can be thought of as an adjunct to reflective methods that allows the administrator to recognize and correct for his or her biases.

In any case, while the administrator who consciously employs these methods may be considered savvy and even wise, one should not expect too much. The human condition is such that, even though this approach is sounder than what usually passes for decision making, it is going to have its share of failures.

Institutionalization

If the kind of reflective scanning of possibilities and consequence analysis suggested is to be very useful in organizations, some sort of institutionalization is required. Having touched on the topic when community opportunities for the expression of values were discussed, here the focus will be on institutionalization within the organization.

To institutionalize something is to routinize it, to install it as part of the social fabric and ongoing activity of the organization. It is helpful to think of two aspects of institutionalization: cultural and bureaucratic. The first is concerned with shared meanings, values, and norms, the second with more formalized practices and procedures. An internal organizational culture that valued the scientific temper and treated ideas as hypotheses would be doubly desirable in that it would be self-critical and educative as befits a school organization, and it would avoid the narrow, conformity-oriented, repressive features that mark so many cultures. The attitudes and values of such an educative culture have already been elaborated in the abstract. Suffice it to say they would be consistent with the following kinds of comments: "We're always looking for good ideas," "Part of our job is to think of ways to improve things around here," "We try to figure out whether something will work ahead of time," "We check things out and debug them," "We're not afraid to criticize ideas," and "If something doesn't work, we change it." Such comments suggest the kind of culture that would be likely to at least encourage the habitual use of reflective methods, that is, their internalization by members of the organization.

More formal practices and procedures might be characteristic of decision making in such small group settings as administrative cabinets, school councils, advisory committees, staff meetings, and ad hoc bodies of various kinds. Practices and procedures can range from setting up a few ground rules to the assignment of special roles such as devil's advocate. Consequence analysis can be facilitated by simple "What Can Go Wrong" sessions or by elaborate data gathering. To give a personal example, I often employ a scanning strategy based on branches of knowledge and people. This involves exploring possible consequences in psychological, sociological, political, economic, or other disciplinary terms using relevant concepts or theories that come to mind and imagining consequences for various individuals and groups such as faculty, other administrators, students, community members, governing boards, and so on, including key figures and informal cliques or factions. The specific strategies used are not important as long as they free up critical intelligence, not a small thing in settings where hierarchy, deference, gamesmanship, and hidden agendas often rule the roost.

A danger is that what has been institutionalized will become ritualized. Examples of pitfalls to be avoided include overanalysis and the use of reflective methods when they are inappropriate.[99] With regard to the former, it is clear that not all consequences of decisions are foreseeable and that reasonable action can be mired in the quicksands of unreasonable efforts to be thorough. With regard to the latter, it is important to recognize that a great deal of human behavior is virtually automatic, a result of impulse, habit, and custom. Such behavior typically works well over a wide spectrum of social relations. A whole host of daily activities can be taken for granted and do not require questioning or critical analysis. The trick, of course, is to be able to identify those that do. Hence, a significant problem in institutionalizing reflective analysis in organizations is knowing when to use it and when to abstain. A more subtle pitfall is allowing the analysis to be driven by available data rather than by more pertinent but more hypothetical information. The ubiquity of computers, so versatile and useful in so many respects, makes this a potential problem in many contemporary organizations. The antidote is to stick with organizational purposes and insist on relevance.

Even if successful institutionalization of formal practices and procedures occurs and even if it is buttressed by the right kinds of school culture and even administrative culture, reflective analysis should never be seen as a panacea or, in its application in the individual case, a sure thing. Simon's concept of *satisficing,* or finding a solution that is good enough, and Lindblom's notion of muddling through both recognize this. But we should expect satisficing at a high level and muddling through with a method.[100]

PROFESSING

Over the years, I have written two pieces explicitly devoted to the professorship in educational administration: a chapter in a 1964 book on the professorship that Jack Culbertson and I edited and a 1983 article in *Educational Administration Quarterly.* Both presented a philosophical position on educational administration more or less consistent with what has been presented here. However, times change. In the 1964 chapter, I argued for the importance of values in educational administration and proposed that observational studies be given high priority because of their connection to and relevance for administrative life. I also called for investigations of the professional culture of school administrators and the teacher culture in the social context of the school. Today, all of those things are mainstream thinking—not, of course, because I and others wrote as we did so long ago, but for many reasons, including the influences of societal changes and the social sciences on educational administration. The 1983 article also dealt with some of the practical issues of professing and the departmental context, especially in what were then downtimes in terms of resources. Today, resources are still quite limited, but, partly as a result of a spate of national reports, including one directly on educational administration, there is considerable discussion and some action on program reform. Even though

McCarthy and her associates interpreted their data on the professorship as showing satisfaction and complacency, the times seem riper for change than they have for many years, clearly much more so than in 1983 when so much energy was being expended on the management of decline.[101]

Most recommendations for reform in preparation programs focus narrowly on curriculum and advocate a stronger clinical emphasis. Insofar as such an emphasis means that serious attention is to be given to the problems of practice and to the preparation of practitioners who will be able to deal with those problems effectively, one can only applaud it. At the same time, a clinical emphasis has the potential for all sorts of unintended consequences that could easily produce worse, not better, programs. The examination of inquiry, values, and praxis already undertaken is full of implications for programs and for professing.

Programs

When I first studied educational administration and in my early years as a teacher of that subject, the field was dominated by the same general kind of clinical emphasis now being proposed. The practice-oriented professors of that time commonly dispensed a combination of lore, recipes, personal experiences and bias, what I previously referred to as the pontifications of great men and, of course, they were virtually all men. Still, these were often men of wit and wisdom, well educated, accomplished, and respected. One problem was that they were not theorists in the sense of being interested in explanation. They didn't ask why and how things worked. Steeped in the situational contingencies of their own experience, they taught what worked for them. Sometimes, conflicting advice was heard from different professors: For instance, "Don't make big changes the first year. Stop, look, and listen; get to know the school and community before you innovate." and "Strike while the iron is hot. People expect a new administrator to make changes. Move while you're still in the honeymoon period." If there wasn't too much conflicting advice, this kind of teaching went over well. Many students, neophytes to administration, felt that, at last, they were getting some straight answers from professors, rather than the traditional "it all depends."

Field experiences and internships of varying degrees of formality were often noteworthy parts of these programs. Grounded in old boys' networks built by professors and school administrators, these activities served important socializing functions. However, the programs were geared to norms of reciprocity. The university got a training site, the schools gained a willing worker, and the student was given entry of sorts to the profession. On the program side, the students were defined as guests and reminded to look and behave accordingly. What was learned was heavily dependent on the cooperating administrator but was likely to be of the same stripe as the combination of lore and recipes many of the practice-oriented professors propounded. Critical analysis, questioning of current arrangements, or attention to why something was done were ordinarily not emphasized. I vividly recall an end of the school year session at which a dozen or so interns and their administrator-mentors reported. Every one of the interns began with fulsome praise of their mentors and their experiences as tyros in administration. Little of substance was discussed, although many allusions were made to the real world, the firing line, and the like. The afternoon turned out to be a long hymn of praise and thanksgiving as the students, the mentors, and the professors each spoke highly of the other two groups.

There is much to be said for all of this from a sociological point of view: The satisfaction level is high all around, and bonds between the university and the schools are cultivated and strengthened. Yet it is also an intellectual charade, and it seriously underestimates the ability and willingness of educators to come to grips openly and more critically with school problems. Furthermore, other common goals such as school improvement can also forge bonds that are both strong and morally authentic.

Some will surely argue that I sketched a worst case scenario, one that their programs will avoid. I hope so, but I am concerned that, in the rush to more clinically oriented preparation, substance will be neglected and we will get administrators who reproduce what we have now. An obligingly uncritical culture of practice could easily develop in university departments that become so preoccupied with their relationships with schools that those relationships are treated as ends rather than as means to excellence in preparation. In any case, such cultures are hardly a rarity, given the commitment of most professors to practice and their natural empathy for practitioners. The problem is, of course, a classic one in applied fields like educational administration. At issue is the kind of program that, in long-range terms, genuinely serves practice. If we are to aim for school improvement and administrators who can attain it, I believe it is crucial to emphasize the kind of critical practice I have described, morally sensitive and committed to reflective methods. Such practice feeds on a wide array of concepts and ideas, most of which originate in the social sciences.

Hence, it would be a serious mistake to reduce the emphasis on such subject matter in educational administration programs. Obviously, as Campbell and others have insisted, a better job needs to be done applying social science content to the concrete problems of schools and their administration. These problems, rather than the social sciences, constitute the heart of educational administration, but the simple truth is that social science concepts and theories are an enormous resource in dealing with those problems. Indeed, it is difficult to deal intelligently with a serious problem in educational administration without them. They not only furnish ways of seeing that might have been lacking but can also enter into the most elementary kinds of administrator analysis. For instance, estimating how certain individuals or groups will react to a proposal educes, respectively, psychological and sociological concepts.[102]

Clearly, students of educational administration need a solid familiarity with a stock of social science concepts and theories. This can be gained through courses in both the social sciences and their application-oriented counterparts in educational administration. However, the crux of the preparation program should be situational and concrete. Field experiences are only one suitable device; case studies, simulations, and personal narratives are examples of others that can be used in an increasingly wide array of media. But these experiences will be exercises in futility unless reflective methods and critical analysis play a key part in them. In teaching such methods, my experience favors a problem-centered, holistic approach that stresses the clarification and critical examination of proposed courses of action in terms of the values they promote and especially of their possible consequences. Consequence analysis is a central feature of the process since it often appears to be crucial to successful problem resolution. The remediation of likely negative consequences as part of a solution can help to avoid a common phenomenon in administration—the solution to one problem creates several new ones.[103]

Whatever the details of the curriculum in an educational administration program, it should be seen in the larger contexts of inquiry and practice. The view taken here emphasizes the continuity of inquiry and practice. The methods and subject matter of the one serve and are tested by the other. Just as professors seek a fuller understanding of how schools work, practitioners seek such understanding for their own situations. Since their schools exhibit individual, contingent characteristics, practitioners need all the conceptual resources they can muster. Practice, as praxis, and inquiry have a symbiotic relationship that preparation programs ought to nurture. If there is to be a greater clinical emphasis in preparation programs that goes beyond rhetoric and recipes, I believe this is the direction it should take.

Professors

Based on the studies by Campbell and Newell and by McCarthy and her associates, along with a more focused investigation of new hires in the field by Daresh, it can be concluded that professors of educational administration are working in smaller programs, but often in larger departments with several other programs, and are satisfied with their career choice and their jobs. The number of female faculty members, but not of minorities, has risen sharply. The average age of faculty has gone up, and at least half will be replaced in the next ten or fifteen years. Recent hires come from a variety of institutions, not just a few prestigious ones and have experience in schools or in administration but not extensive experience and rarely as school superintendents. While more professors are devoting more time to research, the research qualifications of new professors are not of overriding importance in their selection. Preparation programs have continued to proliferate, mainly in nonresearch institutions. Not surprisingly, most faculty rate their own programs very highly.[104]

These studies suggest a variety of issues. Some have been discussed and debated for a long time. Some are more easily resolved than others. For instance, the desirability of better and fewer preparation programs, a recommendation of the 1987 National Commission on Excellence in Educational Administration, has been proposed periodically for years. While everybody favors better programs, the proliferation continues mainly for reasons of politics and institutional adaptation. This is an example of one of the more complex and less easily resolved issues in the field.[105]

The sharp increase in the number of women professors is a long overdue first step in the resolution of the problem of underrepresentation, and this change brings with it a talent pool that promises to be renewable, given the number of women now enrolled in doctoral programs in the field. Recruitment to advanced study and to the professorship continues to need attention, but the focus should now shift to matters of collegiality and socialization, where efforts ought to be made to ensure that women have every opportunity for participation and career development available to men and, at a more subtle level, a genuine welcome to equal partnership in the work of the department and profession. Stemming from steps taken to address a larger problem, this consequent one is an example of the more resolvable type. Departmental commitment to inclusion, mutual support, professionalism, and good colleagueship can make all the difference.

Next, a brief comment on departmental or divisional structure that combines educational administration with other programs, a popular game deans have played for some years now. This organization is a false economy that, in reality, adds a layer of administration and creates new problems of coordination. It is particularly inappropriate for strong programs because it weakens their thrust and activities as resources are devoted to shoring up the weaker ones. Should the proposed reduction in the number of educational administration units actually take place, a doubtful prospect, the larger faculties that would presumably result would be more likely to be organized in a single, uncombined structure, a salutary consequence. As far as the interprogram dialogue that is sometimes claimed as an advantage of a combined department is concerned, I have yet to see evidence that, in the first place, such a structure actually leads to much substantive interaction, and in the second place, that when it does, it is genuinely beneficial. Dialogue based on common interests will occur in universities without hybrid departments. In any case, the written word, not nearby colleagues, is normally the best source of ideas concerning one's research. Moreover, only the most relevant and most expert authors need be consulted. The points made suggest some of the limitations of combined units. At the very least, decisions about departmental structure should not be made or accepted uncritically. They deserve serious consideration by both faculty and administrators.

Research: Cultivating Vitality

The finding that educational administration professors are doing more research was countered by the failure to stress research preparation as an employment criterion and, to some degree, by the reduced salience of the more prestigious institutions in the preparation of professors, which suggests at least the possibility of poorer preparation in research methods. This possibility looms larger for other reasons. The criticisms of science made by neo-Marxists and subjectivists tend to downgrade the importance of research, and the newly popular qualitative studies have a less clear-cut technology than their quantitative counterparts and less obvious requirements. And all of this is occurring in an applied field where research is but one of multiple interests and activities. Given the current conditions, it is essential that the vitality of research in the field be protected and cultivated.

The social sciences are wonderful sources of concepts and theories, but the bulk of the knowledge base in educational administration has emerged as a result of studies of administrators, schools, and their contexts. And make no mistake about it, we know a lot about schools and their administration. Despite the reams of nonsense that have been written on this matter, often by those who see failed science as advantageous to their ideological positions, there are a large number of general propositions relevant to educational administration that are reasonably well supported by the available evidence.

Of course, no science deals with certainty. The statement that nothing is known with absolute certainty as a result of science will always be correct. As has been made clear, science is concerned with plausibility and probability. What counts as knowledge is a matter of making judgments based on the extent to which theory is logical and reasonable and empirical evidence compelling. And, of course, knowledge is ever subject to revision or abandonment by new inquiry.[106] This is the real world of science, which, seen for what it is, provides a storehouse of valuable concepts, theories, and results that constitute a knowledge base and refutes those who claim research has come to naught.

Given the importance of good empirical work to both inquiry and the kind of praxis described earlier, programs that prepare professors should be especially attentive to this aspect of instruction. It can also be hoped that, as scholarship that is more ideological than empirical begins to wane in educational administration, energy and commitment will be transferred to such constructive pursuits as research.

While questions about qualitative methods are currently more salient and more pressing, quantitative methods ought not to be neglected. The sophistication of computer technology has made quantitative studies more vital and valuable than ever. Survey research and instrumented inquiries of various kinds continue to serve the profession well. For instance, the work of Hoy and his associates in updating and extending scholarship on school climates is a major contribution to both researchers and practitioners who now have access to a number of relatively simple measures of organizational openness and health.[107]

There should be room for a variety of styles and types of research in educational administration. Indeed, different problems require different methods. A danger that ought to be guarded against is the belief that any one method can provide all the answers and should be an exclusive vehicle for inquiry.

Field Research

With qualitative studies becoming more and more common in educational administration, one senses both a delight with the medium and a certain uneasiness. The delight appears to be related to the direct way in which this kind of research confronts experience in schools, reinforced by the highly readable character of some of the published accounts of administration and schooling presented by field researchers. The uneasiness probably stems from the greater all-around ambiguity of this kind of research in contrast to quantitative work, abetted by the fact that many professors have had no formal training in field studies.

An element of confusion is added by the different emphases found in different strands of field work. The anthropologists, under the banner of ethnography, stress culture, holistic thinking, and thick description. Socialized to, but nowadays less often experienced in, the traditions of lengthy field stints in faraway primitive societies (often colonies), anthropologists are sometimes quite critical of the use of their methods by others in studies of small segments of modern societies (e.g., organizations) conducted over brief durations. The sociologists, under the rubric of participant (and nonparticipant) observation, focus on social systems and collectivities of all kinds. They are interested in culture, but unlike cultural anthropologists, this type of research is not their principal empirical alternative, and they are less proprietary. Most symbolic interactionists operate under the sociological umbrella but pay special attention to socially constructed reality and the differential enactment of norm-governed behavior. The neo-Marxists, having recently begun to describe their work as critical ethnography, continue to emphasize power and oppression and various societal inequities, especially those that are class based. Subjectivists, perhaps appropriately, are not grouped under a particular label, but most of them are concerned about individual agency and personal travail in social settings, with empathetic understanding often a more important goal than scientific credibility. More oriented to the latter are microethnographers and others concerned with finding ethnographic equivalents to validity, reliability, and other concepts common in quantitative research.[108]

Within each of these emphases can be found further differences. The "humanistic" versus "scientific" one just noted cuts across anthropology and sociology, as well as applied fields. An example of another kind is the disagreement on whether field studies should mainly aim at generating theory or seek both to generate and verify it, a disagreement that occurs largely within the more scientific camp.[109]

While the richness versus rigor debates that have been part of sociology off and on since the 1930s and, more recently, part of education appear to have ended for now in a live and let live draw, the richness advocates seem to be maintaining among themselves the traditions of dispute. Besides all of the disagreements arising from the different emphases just reviewed, the issue of field research crafted to further political agendas promises to heat up. The neo-Marxists have so far been the chief advocates of such research, but it can be conducted by anyone with an ideological axe to grind.[110] Work of this kind will probably not become very extensive but will be concentrated among those few whose ideological commitments are especially intense. It violates scientific norms of impersonal assessment, which most scholars appear to accept, despite the difficulty of fully satisfying them in social science research. Hence, it is likely to have a serious credibility problem and remain highly controversial. Research that makes an ideological position explicit but still strives to adhere to scientific standards will, of course, fare better.

That this issue arises in the context of qualitative studies underscores the limitations and vulnerabilities of methods where the researcher is ordinarily the sole observer, interpreter, and creator of the field notes that eventually become the study's primary sources of data. This point and the representativeness issue have, of course, been raised over and over. Having argued in favor of field research for many years, I nevertheless recognize the validity of such criticisms.[111]

These criticisms lose much of their force when the purpose of field research is to develop hypotheses to be tested later. While I believe that field studies can themselves provide such tests, their special strength lies in the possibilities they present for concept and theory generation. The process of discussing and thinking through alternative interpretations of field data is, for me at least, one of the most creative and enjoyable features of science. It represents a genuine opportunity to make linkages between the concrete phenomena of everyday life and explanation.

Others are quite concerned about testing theory, especially in the light of the popularity of perspectives that do not address that problem. For instance, Hammersley pointed out that British sociology of education has, in recent times, been dominated by two thrusts: neo-Marxism and ethnographic studies inspired by symbolic interactionism. He argued that, because neither emphasizes the testing of theory, there has not been an accumulation of theoretical knowledge, a situation he described as a dismal performance. A different kind of criticism was made by Stimson. He argued that there is a tendency to limit field work to one medium, speech. He saw this as a serious shortcoming that ignored all of the nonverbal features of the setting including physical arrangements, furnishings, clothing, various props, and nonverbal human communication. Stimson noted that these features of the setting send their own messages. His point is the one-sidedness of most current observational work in its preoccupation with talk and neglect of artifacts and physical symbols, a point that should be taken to heart in educational administration, which has shared that preoccupation and neglect.[112]

All of this suggests that there is an array of general approaches to field research and a number of broad issues. Many of the issues are of a kind that are rarely settled by intellectual argument since in the end they depend on values and preferences. A certain settlement by usage does occur, however, as researchers opt for or against, for instance, work that is explicitly and extensively ideological.

The general impression is one of disagreement and some disarray. Even the names for such studies range over *field, qualitative, ethnographic, observational, natural setting,* and more.[113] How then should educational administration programs address the need for adequate preparation in this sort of research? There appears to be no single best answer to this question. The aim is straightforward, to provide knowledge about field methods and competence in their use. The nightmare scenario is that of a professor with only a little knowledge sending untrained or poorly trained graduate students armed with notepads and tape recorders into the field.

If departments of sociology or anthropology offer courses on field methods open to nonmajors, this is obviously a desirable alternative. Experts and good courses on field studies can be found in other social science or applied social science departments in the university as well but usually have to be searched out. Schools of education are just beginning to look at more systematic ways to provide this kind of preparation. It has no obvious departmental home and currently is often taught by professors who are interested and knowledgeable whatever their substantive specialization. There are no good reasons to object to this, provided the professors are genuinely well trained, experienced, and legitimated by publication of this kind of research.

To be avoided are professors who wish mainly to carry on a crusade against quantitative research or spend a whole course on the kind of issues I earlier described as rarely settled by argument. Happily, there is a saving grace amid the debates and disarray. It is that field research does have a subject matter that is concrete and to the point. As in the study of quantitative methods, this subject matter is geared to the provision of information that can facilitate the process of decision making in research. Decisions, for instance, about which research site to study; about gaining access to that site; about what to observe; about whom to talk with and what to ask them; about what kind of materials to request; about how to record data; about how to classify and interpret the data collected; about how to check impressions, interpretations, and tentative explanations derived from early observations in later ones and through other people; about how to disengage properly from the research site, and about how to write up the results of the study. Also important is the consideration of ethical questions involved in this kind of research, especially in connection with the protection of the people and organization that participated. Nor should the broader issues discussed earlier be ignored: it's just that they should not be covered to the point where specific methodological strategies and techniques are given short shrift. I believe that interviewing methods should also be part of this preparation. Almost all field research involves interviewing of one kind or another, and an increasing number of studies done in educational administration are based entirely on the interview as a data-gathering device.

In any event, advanced preparation programs should now include training in qualitative research methods just as they have in quantitative ones. Such training is essential for those who contemplate field research, but it also can sharpen the observational, information-collecting, and interpretive skills of practitioners. Indeed, one writer recently suggested a number of parallels in the work of educational administrators and ethnographers, including concern about holistic vision or the big picture.[114]

administration represents a lost opportunity of some magnitude given the number produced. That so many professors supervise dozens of completely unrelated dissertations over their careers is probably symptomatic of the field's uneven commitment to scholarship. In any case, it serves the field badly.

Needless to say, professors of practice should also mount research programs. Their area of interest is rife with possibilities for study: from socialization to decision making to effective preparation for administrative practice. Such research could be of great importance to the field.

All this should help build a departmental culture that fosters commitments to inquiry and its uses. Such a culture can accommodate any scholarship that is open to critical assessment and revision and would, of course, benefit from a diversity of theoretical and methodological orientations among its faculty. Educational administration departments of the kind sketched here will be vital and exciting places to work for professors and they will be places that honor their obligations to both inquiry and practice.

CHAPTER 3
Concluding Comments

I have tried to put intellectual developments in educational administration in perspective. Specifically examined were the philosophical and social science origins of neo-Marxist critical theory and subjectivism, two viewpoints that took root in the social sciences and then educational administration and are already waning in the social sciences. In educational administration, their main project has been the criticism of science. Because their criticisms have been stereotypic and showed little or no understanding of science as it is practiced by people, I went to some length to describe science as it is, a very human activity grounded in curiosity, openness, skepticism, and a desire to test rather than merely accept ideas. Cast in the Deweyan context of inquiry, the reflective methods of science are seen to contrast sharply with dogmatic, self-righteous, and closed thinking of every stripe.

I recommended that such methods inform educational administration programs in their activities geared to both practice and research. In the rush to more clinical preparation programs just how practice is to be improved has not been given sufficient thought. The processes of inquiry seem to be a key if the aim is administrators whose decision making is based on the critical and reflective assessment of alternatives. Furthermore, such assessment serves moral choice, which must be seen in the context of real situations that require estimates of the likelihood of selected options actually serving desired ends—hence the concept of praxis or thoughtful, informed practice.

Inquiry in educational administration should be upgraded, not downgraded as it has been by science bashers who seem devoted to the politicalization of research or to relativism, two modern versions of alchemy. Actually, when it comes to doing research, most scholars in the social sciences and educational administration have shown a fundamental wisdom. For instance, Smelser noted that "attacks on sociological empiricism have not been very successful; the vast majority of those engaged in actual sociological research . . . adhere to a kind of theoretically eclectic empiricist perspective," and he added that when what he called phenomenological or Marxist critics conduct empirical research, they face some of the same issues as other researchers and turn to scientific methods. In educational administration, Culbertson concluded that the field's scholars "still look to science . . . for a legitimating cloak, facilitator of inquiry, and a tool." Griffiths came to the same conclusion in his review of organizational studies in educational administration.[118] The simple truth is that the practical empiricism of scientific method works.

A concern that appears to stem from stereotypic views of science suggests that a commitment to inquiry cuts one off from emotion, passion, or sensitivity to behavior that is irrational or unpredictable. This concern ignores the fact that most of what is known about emotion comes courtesy of psychological science. It is true, of course, that irrationality is studied using rational methods, but the burden of proof clearly lies with those who might have an alternative in mind.[119] It is worth noting that field research, now in fairly wide use in educational administration, represents a set of rational methods that can furnish insights into the emotional, symbolic, and irrational sides of administrative and school life. However, there seems to be little danger that irrationality will be neglected. After all, there is plenty of it around.

Another question sometimes asked about philosophies that stress inquiry and reflective methods is whether they can secure the kind of emotional commitment needed to sustain their use in real situations. The response is that this is not an insurmountable problem since reflective methods can be internalized by people and institutionalized by organizations.[120] Furthermore, when one looks at the religious, ethnic, racial, and cultural exclusivity and intolerance that result from unquestioned beliefs and commitments, one can easily become emotional about reflective methods. The same can be said in connection with our social institutions. For instance, political expediency and special interests seem to rule the roost in government as greed does in business. Is it too much to hope that education could do better, that decisions there could more frequently be based on critical, reflective thinking that assesses alternatives, consequences, and the purposes they serve? School administrators are in a position to be exemplars in this regard, something that helps set an agenda for preparation programs in educational administration. From my point of view, that agenda is both intellectually and emotionally appealing.

[1]On the historical background see R. F. Campbell, "The professorship in educational administration: A personal view," *Educational Administration Quarterly,* 17(1981):1–24; R. F. Campbell, T. Fleming, L. J. Newell and J. W. Bennion, *A history of thought and practice in educational administration.* New York: Teachers College Press, 1987; H. A. Moore, Jr., "The ferment in school administration," in D. E. Griffiths (Ed.), *Behavioral science and educational administration,* The Sixty-third Yearbook of the National Society for the Study of Education. Chicago: University of Chicago Press, 1964.

[2]For a review of much of this scholarship, see N. J. Boyan (Ed.), *Handbook of research on educational administration,* New York: Longman, 1988.

[3]See N. J. Boyan, "A study of the formal and informal organization of a school faculty," unpublished doctoral dissertation, Harvard University, 1951. An example of one of the many calls for more ethnographic-style research is D. E. Griffiths, *Administrative theory,* New York: Appleton-Century-Crofts, 1959, p. 35.

[4]On theories of the middle range, see R. K. Merton, *Social theory and social structure.* New York: Free Press, 1968, especially pp. 39–72.

[5]See, for example, L. W. Downey and F. Enns (Eds.), *The social sciences and educational administration.* Edmonton, Canada: University of Alberta and University Council for Educational Administration, 1963; and D. E. Tope (Ed.), *The social sciences view school administration.* Englewood Cliffs, NJ: Prentice Hall, 1965.

[6]R. F. Campbell, "What peculiarities in educational administration make it a special case?" in A. W. Halpin (Ed.), *Administrative theory in education,* Chicago: Midwest Administration Center, University of Chicago, 1958; J. Culbertson, R. H. Farquhar, B. M.

Forgarty and M. R. Shibles (Eds.), *Social science content for preparing educational leaders.* Columbus, OH: Charles E. Merrill, 1973; K. Goldhammer, *The social sciences and the preparation of educational administrators.* Edmonton, Canada: University of Alberta and University Council for Educational Administration, 1963.

[7]For example, R. H. Farquhar, *The humanities in preparing educational administrators.* Eugene, OR: ERIC Clearinghouse on educational administration, State-of-the-Knowledge Series 7, 1970; O. B. Graff and C. M. Street, "Developing a value framework for educational administration," in R. F. Campbell and R. T. Gregg (Eds.), *Administrative behavior in education,* New York: Harper, 1957; R. E. Ohm and W. G. Monahan (Eds.), *Educational administration: Philosophy in action.* Norman, OK: University of Oklahoma, 1965.

[8]See, for example, J. A. Culbertson, P. B. Jacobson and T. L. Reller, *Administrative relationships, a case book.* Englewood Cliffs, NJ: Prentice Hall, 1960; S. P. Hencley (Ed.), *The Internship in administrative preparation.* Columbus, OH and Washington: University Council for Educational Administration and the Committee for the Advancement of School Administration, 1963; C. G. Sargent and E. L. Belisle, *Educational administration: Cases and concepts.* New York: Houghton Mifflin, 1955.

[9]D. J. Leu. and H. C. Rudman (Eds.), *Preparation programs for school administrators: Common and specialized learnings.* East Lansing, MI: Michigan State University, 1963.

[10]R. F. Campbell and L. J. Newell, *A study of professors of educational administration.* Columbus, OH: University Council for educational administration, 1973. For more recent data, see M. M. McCarthy, G. D. Kuh, L. J. Newell and C. M. Iacona, *Under scrutiny: The educational administration professoriate.* Tempe, AZ: University Council for Educational Administration, 1988.

[11]For a study of textbooks see T. E. Glass (Ed.), *An analysis of texts on school administration 1820–1985.* Danville, IL: Interstate, 1986.

[12]For a discussion of the effort to make educational administration more scientific see J. A. Culbertson, "A century's quest for a knowledge base," in Boyan, *Handbook of research on educational administration.*

[13]For example, A. W. Halpin, "Administrative theory: The fumbled touch," in A. M. Kroll (Ed.), *Issues in American education,* New York: Oxford University Press, 1970; G. L. Immegart, "The Study of Educational Administration, 1954–1974," in L. L. Cunningham, W. G. Hack and R. O. Nystrand (Eds.), *Educational administration: The developing decades,* Berkeley, CA: McCutchan, 1977; C. G. Miskel and T. Sandlin, "Survey research in educational administration," *Educational Administration Quarterly,* 17 (1981):1–20.

[14]*Administrative Science Quarterly,* which began publication in 1956 reflects this orientation.

[15]N. J. Boyan, "Follow the leader: Commentary on research in educational administration," *Educational Researcher,* 10(1981):6–13; D. J. Willower, "Synthesis and Projection," in Boyan, *Handbook of research on educational administration.*

[16]A few parts of this section draw on my entry in M. C. Alkin (Ed.), *Encyclopedia of educational research.* New York: Macmillan, 1992.

[17]An instructive source on the situation in one social science is N. J. Smelser (Ed.), *Handbook of sociology.* Newbury Park, CA: Sage, 1988.

[18]I. Wallerstein, "Marxisms as utopias: Evolving ideologies," *American Journal of Sociology,* 91(1986):1302.

[19]On the latter see J. E. Roemer, Ed. *Analytical Marxism.* Cambridge, England: Cambridge University Press, 1986. For a critical treatment from a more orthodox perspective, see M. A. Lebowitz, "Is 'Analytical Marxism' Marxism?" *Science and Society,* 52(1988): 191–214.

[20]See H. Garfinkel, *Studies in ethnomethodology,* Englewood Cliffs, NJ: Prentice Hall, 1967; P. K. Manning, "Existential sociology," *Sociological Quarterly,* 14(1973):200–225; A. Schutz, *The phenomenology of the social world,* Evanston, IL: Northwestern University Press, 1967.

[21]See D. Martindale's examination of symbolic interactionism for a treatment of Mead and other earlier contributors. *The nature and types of sociological theory,* Boston: Houghton Mifflin, 1960, pp. 339–375. A major work by H. Blumer is *Symbolic interactionism,* Englewood

Cliffs, NJ: Prentice Hall, 1969. N. J. Smelser's comment is in his chapter on "Social structure," in Smelser, *Handbook of sociology*, p. 122.

[23]D. Held, *Introduction to critical theory: Horkheimer to Habermas*, Berkeley and Los Angeles: University of California Press, 1980, p. 13. Another excellent history is M. Jay, *The dialectical imagination: A history of the Frankfurt School and the Institute for Social Research, 1923–1950*, Boston: Little, Brown, 1973.

[24]On the new sociology, see J. Karabel and A. H. Halsey (Eds.), *Power and ideology in education*, New York: Oxford University Press, 1977; and M. F. D. Young (Ed.), *Knowledge and control: New directions for the sociology of education*, London: Collier-Macmillan, 1971. An influential American study, done from an economics perspective was S. Bowles and H. Gintis, *Schooling in capitalist America*, New York: Basic Books, 1976.

[24]Quoted in Held, *Introduction to critical theory*, p. 191.

[25]W. P. Foster, "Administration and the crisis in legitimacy," *Harvard Educational Review*, 50(1980):496–505. See also Foster's, *Paradigms and promises*, Buffalo, NY: Prometheus, 1986. H. A. Simon's classic work in administration is *Administrative behavior*, New York: Macmillan, 1958.

[26]R. J. Bates, "Educational administration, the sociology of science and the management of knowledge," *Educational Administration Quarterly*, 16(1980):1–20.

[27]See, for instance, Foster, *Paradigms and promises*; H. A. Giroux, *Critical theory and educational practice*, Geelong, Australia: Deakin University, 1963.

[28]See G. L. Anderson, "Critical ethnography in education: Origins, current status, and new directions," *Review of Educational Research*, 59(1989):249–270; R. A. Quantz and T. W. O'Connor, "Writing critical ethnography: Dialogue, multivoicedness, and carnival in cultural texts," *Educational Theory*, 38(1988):95–109.

[29]On institutional theory see J. W. Meyer and B. Rowan, "Institutionalized organizations: Formal structure as myth and ceremony," *American Journal of Sociology*, 83(1977):340–363 and J. W. Meyer and W. R. Scott, *Organizational environments: Ritual and rationality*, Beverly Hills, CA: Sage, 1983. W. W. Waller's classic in education is *The sociology of teaching*, New York: Wiley, 1932.

[30] H. A. Giroux, "Theories of reproduction and resistance in the new sociology of education," *Harvard Educational Review,* 53(1983): 257–293.

[31] P. Willis, *Learning to labor,* Lexington, MA: Heath, 1977.

[32] See B. Agger, "Marxism 'or' the Frankfurt school?" *Philosophy of the Social Sciences,* 13(1983):347–365 and sources he cites.

[33] Giroux, *Critical theory and educational practice.*

[34] H. A. Giroux and P. McLaren, "Teacher education as a counterpublic sphere: Radical pedagogy as a form of cultural politics," *Philosophy and Social Criticism,* 1(1987):51–69.

[35] H. A. Giroux and P. McLaren, "Teacher education as a counterpublic sphere: Radical pedagogy as a form of cultural politics," *Philosophy and Social Criticism,* 1(1987):55.

[36] H. A. Giroux and P. McLaren, "Teacher education as a counterpublic sphere: Radical pedagogy as a form of cultural politics," *Philosophy and Social Criticism,* 1(1987):63.

[37] See E. Husserl, *Ideas: General introduction to pure phenomenology,* W. R. B. Gibson, Trans. New York: Macmillan, 1931; M. Farber, *The foundation of phenomenology,* Cambridge, MA: Harvard University Press, 1943; and *Naturalism and subjectivism.* Springfield, IL: Charles C. Thomas, 1959.

[38] H. P. Rickman, "Science and hermeneutics," *Philosophy of the Social Sciences,* 20(1990):295–316. On Dilthey, see Rickman's *Dilthey Today,* New York: Greenwood, 1988.

[39] D. Vandenberg, "Hermeneutical phenomenology in the study of educational administration," *Journal of Educational Administration,* 20(1982):23–32.

[40] On both writers, see Martindale, *The nature and types of sociological theory.*

[41] J. L. Heap and P. A. Roth, "On phenomenological sociology," *American Sociological Review,* 38(1973):354–367.

[42] For example, see G. Psathas (Ed.), *Phenomenological sociology,* New York: Wiley, 1973; T. W. Wann (Ed.), *Behaviorism and phenomenology,* Chicago: University of Chicago Press, 1964.

[43] One quite typical collection in sociology includes a minimum of seven broad types of theory, eleven if certain distinguishable subtypes are counted. See A. Wells (Ed.), *Contemporary sociological theories,* Santa Monica, CA: Goodyear, 1978.

[44] H. J. Hartley, "Humanistic existentialism and the school administrator," in F. W. Lutz (Ed.), *Toward improved urban education*, Worthington, OH: Charles H. Jones, 1970.

[45] On systems theory see T. B. Greenfield, "Administration and systems analysis," *Canadian Administrator*, 3(1964):25–30. His main subjectivistic works are "Theory about organization: A new perspective and its implications for schools," in M. Hughes (Ed.), *Administering education: International challenge*, London: Athlone, 1975; "Reflections on organization theory and the truths of irreconcilable realities," *Educational Administration Quarterly*, 14(1978):1–23; "The man who comes back through the door in the wall," *Educational Administration Quarterly*, 16(1980):26–59; "Theories of educational organization: A critical perspective," in T. Husen and T. N. Postlewaite (Eds.), *International encyclopedia of education*, Vol. 9. Oxford, England: Pergamon, 1985; "The decline and fall of science in educational administration," *Interchange*, 17(1986):57–80. For commentary on Greenfield by one of his followers, see P. C. Gronn, *Rethinking educational administration: T. B. Greenfield and his critics*, Geelong, Australia: Deakin University, 1983.

[46] The first statement is from "Theory about organization," p. 74; the second is found in "Theories of educational organization: A Critical perspective," p. 5240.

[47] "The decline and fall," p. 61.

[48] See "Reflections on organization theory" and "The man who comes back."

[49] C. Hodgkinson, *Towards a philosophy of administration*, Oxford, England: Basil Blackwell, 1978; and *The philosophy of leadership*, Oxford, England: Basil Blackwell, 1983.

[50] C. W. Evers, "Hodgkinson on ethics and the philosophy of administration," *Educational Administration Quarterly*, 21(1985):27–50.

[51] See, for example, J. J. Blase, "The Micropolitics of the school: The everyday political orientation of teachers toward open school principals," 24(1989):377–407. Blase has also coauthored an article which makes some of the same kinds of sweeping criticisms of social science as Greenfield and offers hermeneutics as a preferred approach. See J. K. Smith and J. J. Blase, "From empiricism to hermeneutics: Educational leadership as a practical and moral activity," *Journal of Educational Administration*, 29(1991):6–21.

[52]Two sources that emphasize rigor in qualitative research are Y. S. Lincoln and E. G. Guba, *Naturalistic inquiry,* Newbury Park, CA: Sage, 1985; and R. G. Owens, "Methodological rigor in naturalistic inquiry: Some issues and answers," *Educational Administration Quarterly,* 18(1982):1–21. The emerging field of quantitative ethnography is another example as are microethnographic studies of, for instance, classroom language. For a specific study see H. Mehan, "Structuring school structure," *Harvard Educational Review,* 48(1978):32–64. A more general source is Part III in J. Green and C. Wallat (Eds.), *Ethnography and language in educational settings,* Norwood, NJ: Ablex, 1981.

[53]See A. W. Hart, "Attribution as effect: An outsider principal's succession," *Journal of Educational Administration,* 26(1988): 331–352; P. C. Gronn, "Talk as the work: The accomplishment of school administration," *Administrative Science Quarterly,* 28(1983):1–21. A. R. Thomas, "Seeing isn't believing? Neither is hearing," *Educational Administration Quarterly,* 22(1986): 29–48, is a criticism of Gronn's study.

[54]See R. B. Everhart, "Fieldwork methodology in educational administration," in Boyan, *Handbook of research on educational administration*; and Willower, "Synthesis and projection."

[55]The F Scale was employed as part of a large project on prejudice that included scholars outside of the Frankfurt school. See Held, *Introduction to critical theory,* and Jay, *The dialectical imagination.* A major work is T. W. Adorno, E. Frenkel-Brunswick, D. J. Levinson and R. N. Sanford, *The authoritarian personality,* New York: Harper, 1950.

[56]The reference to T. S. Kuhn is *The structure of scientific revolutions,* Chicago: University of Chicago Press, 1970. Kuhn has been criticized for his failure to recognize cumulative results in science, and chided for the numerous meanings he gives the word paradigm. For postmodernism (or poststructuralism, especially when French thought is emphasized), see J. Derrida, *Speech and phenomena,* Evanston, IL: Northwestern University Press, 1973; M. Foucault, *Language, counter-memory, practice,* Ithaca, NY: Cornell University Press, 1977; J. F. Lyotard, *The postmodern condition* Manchester, England: Manchester University Press, 1984.

[57]R. Cooper and G. Burrell, "Modernism, postmodernism and organizational analysis: An introduction," *Organization Studies,* 9(1988):91–112.

[58]In educational administration, see for example, F. I. Ortiz and C. Marshall, "Women in educational administration," in Boyan, *Handbook of research on educational administration*; C. Richards, "The search for equity in educational administration," in Boyan, ibid.; C. Shakeshaft, *Women in educational administration*, Newbury Park, CA: Sage, 1987; L. A. Valverde and F. Brown, "Influences on leadership development among racial and ethnic minorities," in Boyan, ibid.

[59]The social science literature is full of writing of this sort. For a classic in sociology see R. S. Lynd, *Knowledge for what? The place of social science in American culture*, Princeton, NJ: Princeton University Press, 1939. On educational administration see, for example, A. W. Halpin, "Ways of Knowing," in R. F. Campbell and J. M. Lipham (Eds.), *Administrative theory as a guide to action*, Chicago: Midwest Administration Center, University of Chicago, 1960; R. J. Hills, "Some notes on the methodology of science for researchers and administrators in education," in W. G. Monahan (Ed.), *Theoretical dimensions of educational administration*, New York: Macmillan, 1975; D. J. Willower, "Schools, values and educational inquiry," *Educational Administration Quarterly*, 9(1973):1–18.

[60]D. Martindale, "Limits of and alternatives to functionalism in sociology," in D. Martindale (Ed.), *Functionalism in the social sciences*, Philadelphia: American academy of political and social science, 1965. The first quotation is from p. 145. The comments on Parsons are on p. 155. The reference to G. Burrell and G. Morgan is, *Sociological paradigms and organizational analysis*, London, Heinemann, 1979.

[61]Criticisms of Marxism run the gamut from John Dewey's analysis of the Marxian dialectic as Hegelian metaphysics to quite comprehensive treatments as found, for example, in T. Rockmore, J. G. Colbert, W. J. Gavin and T. J. Blakely, *Marxism and alternatives*, Dordrecht, Holland: D. Reidel, 1981. A work with much criticism but also some defense that gives a useful picture of debate on Marxism is G. H. R. Parkinson (Ed.), *Marx and Marxism*, Cambridge, England: Cambridge University Press, 1982. The histories of the Frankfurt School by Held and Jay also include many criticisms made of critical theory. In educational administration see G. Lakomski, "Critical Theory and educational administration,"

Journal of Educational Administration, 24(1987): 85 – 100; and my "Marxian critical theory and educational administration: A criticism," *Organizational Theory Dialogue,* (1987, February), pp. 1 – 7.

[62] On the empirical testing of Marxist ideology in education, see D. P. Liston, "Faith and evidence: Examining Marxist explanations of schools," *American Journal of Education,* 96(1988): 323 – 349. A specific study is G. Colclough and E. M. Beck, "The American educational structure and the reproduction of social class," *Sociological Inquiry,* 56(1986): 456 – 476. A review of research on status origins is C. E. Bidwell and N. E. Friedkin, "The sociology of education" in Smelser, *Handbook of sociology.*

[63] The classic on pluralist politics is, of course, R. A. Dahl, *Who governs: Democracy and power in an American city,* New Haven, CT: Yale University Press, 1961. For reviews in educational administration see M. Burlingame, "The politics of education and educational policy: The local level"; and D. E. Mitchell, "Educational politics and policy: The state level," both in Boyan, *Handbook of research on educational administration.*

[64] Anderson, "Critical ethnography," raises the issue and cites a number of relevant sources.

[65] Held, *Introduction to critical theory.* This author adds that while critical theory was an effort to reinvigorate and develop Marxism, orthodox Marxists believed it deemphasized economic concreteness and class struggle, that it was more academic than participative, "On Marxism, rather than in Marxism." See p. 356.

[66] For the flavor of these criticisms in sociology as well as the response to them see L. A. Coser, "Two methods in search of a substance," *American Sociological Review,* 40(1975): 691 – 700; and D. H. Zimmerman, "A reply to Professor Coser," *American Sociologist,* 11(1976): 4 – 13. For a neo-Marxist critique of subjectivist thought in social science and education, see M. Sarap, *Marxism and education,* London: Routeledge and Kegan Paul, 1978.

[67] See, for example, C. W. Evers, "Philosophical research in educational administration," in R. J. S. Macpherson (Ed.), *Ways and meanings of research in educational administration,* Armidale, Australia: University of New England Press, 1987; D. E. Griffiths, "Some thoughts about theory in educational administration," *UCEA Review,* 17(1975): 12 – 18; R. J. Hills, "A critique of Greenfield's

new perspective," *Educational Administration Quarterly,* 16(1980):20−44; G. Lakomski, "The cultural perspective in educational administration," in Macpherson, ibid.; D. J. Willower, "Philosophy and the Study of educational administration," *Journal of Educational Administration,* 23(1985):5−22.

[68]G. Lakomski, "Theory, values and relevance in educational administration," in F. Rizvi (Ed.), *Working papers in ethics and educational administration,* Deakin, Australia: Deakin University, 1985, and "Values and decisionmaking in educational administration," *Educational Administration Quarterly,* 23(1987):70−82.

[69]J. C. Alexander, "The new theoretical movement," in Smelser, *Handbook of Sociology,* p. 77.

[70]D. E. Griffiths, "Intellectual turmoil in educational administration," *Educational Administration Quarterly,* 15(1979):45−65.

[71]Unlike Marxism and phenomenology which stem from single, seminal thinkers, pragmatism is traditionally associated with four philosophers, all Americans: C. S. Peirce, William James, G. H. Mead, and John Dewey. Some writers feel compelled to use the prefix *neo* for most recent writing. I have avoided it in connection with pragmatism because the original versions seem to me to be open and varied enough to accommodate my positions. Dewey's instrumentalism is perhaps the best known version of pragmatism. *His logic: The theory of inquiry,* New York: Henry Holt, 1938 is one of Dewey's more comprehensive works. I have occasionally called my views a mix of naturalism and instrumentalism. Popular usages of the word pragmatism make it a potentially confusing designation.

[72]See my "Philosophy and the study of educational administration."

[73]See for example, R. K. Merton, *The sociology of science,* Chicago: University of Chicago Press, 1973; H. Zuckerman, "The sociology of science," in Smelser, *Handbook of sociology.*

[74]H. F. Wolcott, *The man in the principal's office,* New York: Holt, Rinehart and Winston, 1973. See also R. Rist, "Blitzkrieg ethnography: On the transformation of a method into a movement," *Educational Researcher,* 9(1980):8−10.

[75]Willis, *Learning to labor.* This research is not, strictly speaking, in educational administration. However, it is closely related and has

been widely discussed in the field. See, for example, Everhart, "Fieldwork methodology"; and Foster, *Paradigms and promises.*

[76] See H. I. Brown, "Normative epistemology and naturalized epistemology," *Inquiry,* 31(1988):53–78.

[77] The classical formulation is found in K. Marx and F. Engels, *Correspondence,* D. Torr, (Ed.) and Trans. New York: International Publishers, 1936. For a treatment of the implications of dialectical analysis for organizational studies see J. K. Benson, "Organizations: A dialectical view," *Administrative Science Quarterly,* 22(1977):1–16.

[78] Farber, *The Foundation of phenomenology,* which incidentally is subtitled "Edmund Husserl and the quest for a rigorous science of philosophy" is an excellent interpretation by a philosopher who studied in Europe with Husserl and was founding editor of *Philosophy and Phenomenological Research.* Farber was my advisor for both the bachelor's and master's degrees at Buffalo and I served as his graduate assistant. My studies with him and others at the University convinced me that phenomenological analysis was no more or less than a mental exercise using rules such as bracketing that one hoped would lead to essential insights. Nothing I have learned since suggests any special magic beyond that.

[79] A frequently cited source on hermeneutics not yet noted is H. G. Gadamer, *Truth and method,* New York: Seabury, 1975.

[80] R. Rorty, *Philosophy and the mirror of nature,* Princeton, NJ: Princeton University Press, 1979. See also R. Bubner, "Hermeneutics: Understanding or edification," *Philosophical Topics,* 12(1981): 37–48.

[81] Smith and Blase, "From empiricism to hermeneutics."

[82] H. P. Rickman, "Science and hermeneutics." The first quotation is from pp. 314–315. The rest are from p. 295.

[83] Interestingly and perhaps ironically to some, phenomenological analysis and hermeneutics share a commitment to logical, deductive thought processes with analytic philosophy, sometimes thought of as a modern version of logical positivism.

[84] R. Collins, "Looking forward or looking back? Reply to Denzin," *American Journal of Sociology,* 93(1987):180–184. The quoted material is from pp. 180–181.

[85] Collins, "Looking forward," p. 181.

[86] Values are often defined as conceptions of the desirable. See, for example, the chapter by C. Kluckholn and his colleagues, "Values and value orientations" in the *Theory of action,* in T. Parsons and E. A. Shils (Eds.), *Toward a general theory of action,* Cambridge, MA: Harvard University Press, 1951, p. 395.

[87] This vision need not originate with the administrator. It could be initiated by teachers, parents, the school board, or any of many sources or combinations. The point is that the administrator is now attempting to implement it.

[88] On this issue in John Dewey's thought, see S. Hook, "The place of John Dewey in modern thought," in M. Farber (Ed.), *Philosophic thought in France and the United States,* Buffalo, NY: University of Buffalo Publications in Philosophy, 1950; Dewey himself stated, "Honesty, industry, temperance, justice . . . are not goods to be possessed as they would be if they expressed fixed ends to be attained. They are directions of change in the quality of experience. Growth itself is the only moral 'end.' " See *Reconstruction in philosophy,* Boston: Beacon, 1948, p. 177. At the same time, Dewey pointed out that moral knowledge like other knowledge is cumulative and certain principles gain credibility because experience shows their utility in solving moral problems. Such principles can serve as a directive standard, but are not fixed or absolute and cannot be the final arbiter for the particular case. See J. Dewey and J. H. Tufts, *Ethics,* New York: Henry Holt, 1932, p. 230.

[89] J. Dewey, *Human nature and conduct,* Modern Library Edition. New York: Henry Holt, 1922, p. 278.

[90] Most of these studies used versions of the structured observation technique first reported in H. Mintzberg, *The nature of managerial work,* New York: Harper and Row, 1973. Many of the studies of school administrators are cited and some criticisms of this type of work are presented in my "School organizations: Perspectives in juxtaposition," *Educational Administration Quarterly,* 18(1982): 89–110. Studies of verbal behavior include Gronn, "Talk as the work"; and P. V. Bredeson, "Principally speaking: An analysis of the interpersonal communications of school principals," *Journal of Educational Administration,* 25(1987):55–71.

[91] There are numerous studies of school administrators' attitudes about their work. An example of one of the more comprehensive ones is

L. L. Cunningham and J. T. Hentges, *The American school superintendency, 1982: A summary report,* Arlington, VA: American Association of School Administrators, 1982. A number of the review chapters in Boyan, *Handbook of research on educational administration,* especially the ones by E. Miklos, and N. J. Boyan, are relevant. On stress see A. R. Thomas, "The school and occupational stress," in E. Hoyle and A. McMahon (Eds.), *The management of schools,* London: Kogan-Page, 1986. On humor see C. T. Burford, "Humor of principals and its impact on teachers and the school," *Journal of Educational Administration,* 25(1987): 29–54; and T. R. Kippeny and D. J. Willower, "Humor, peers and the school superintendent," *Administrator's Notebook,* 34(8, 1990):1–4. On vulnerability and organizational protection see A. Blumberg and P. Blumberg, *The school superintendent: Living with conflict,* New York: Teachers College Press, 1985; and G. A. Ziolkowski and D. J. Willower, "School superintendents, crisis management and institutional organizations theory," *Journal of Educational Administration,* 29(1991):50–60, and sources cited therein.

[92]The last two studies cited in endnote 91 are examples of work showing the importance of stragegy and tactics. On the "in-basket" research see J. K. Hemphill, "Personal variables and administrative styles," in Griffiths, *Behavioral science and educational administration.* The full study is J. K. Hemphill, D. E. Griffiths and N. Fredericksen, *Administrative performance and personality,* New York: Teachers College Press, 1962. The expert-typical comparison is K. A. Leithwood and M. Stager, "Expertise in principals' problem solving," *Educational Administration Quarterly,* 25(1989):126–161.

[93]The classic is, of course, Simon's *Administrative behavior.* An excellent review is S. Estler, "Decision making," in Boyan, *Handbook of research on educational administration.* On organized anarchy and the garbage can, the most frequently cited source is J. G. March and J. P. Olsen, *Ambiguity and choice in organizations,* Bergen, Norway: Universitetsforlaget, 1979. In their recent review chapter, H. E. Aldrich and P. V. Marsden stated that while this approach "attracted attention and critical praise . . . when first proposed . . . it has not generated a great deal of research." See "Environments and organizations," in Smelser, *Handbook of sociology.*

[94]H. A. Simon, "Making Management Decisions: The Role of intuition and emotion," *Academy of Management Executive,* February 1987, pp. 57−64. The quotations are from p. 61. See also Simon's, *The sciences of the artificial.* Cambridge, MA: MIT Press, 1979.

[95]D. L. Clark, "Emerging paradigms in organizational theory and research," in Y. S. Lincoln (Ed.), *Organization theory and inquiry,* Beverly Hills, CA: Sage, 1985, p. 77. The term logic-in-use was employed by A. Kaplan in his analysis of processes and suppositions in research. See *The conduct of inquiry,* San Francisco: Chandler, 1964.

[96]My account of deliberation more or less follows John Dewey's. See especially his *Human nature and conduct* and *Logic: The theory of inquiry.* My rendering differs from Dewey's in that it is more explicit about the utility of social science concepts and theories and in its emphasis on an administrative and organizational context.

[97]Dewey, *Human nature and conduct,* p. 190.

[98]On the concept of robustness see my "Reason, robustness and educational administration," Holloway lecture series. Buffalo, NY: Society of educational administrators of Western New York, University at Buffalo, 1975; and J. W. Licata and B. L. Johnson, "Toward a synthesis of inquiry on environmental robustness," *Planning and changing,* 20(1989):215−230, and the sources cited therein. The concepts of habit and character are developed in Dewey, *Human nature and conduct.*

[99]While overanalysis is a potential pitfall in the use of reflective methods, the underanalysis represented by failure to use them is, of course, a more common and a more serious problem.

[100]On school culture, see W. A. Firestone and H. D. Corbett, "Planned organizational change," in Boyan, *Handbook of research on educational administration.* On administrator culture see R. Papalewis, "A case study in organizational culture: Administrators' shared values, perceptions, and beliefs," *Planning and Changing,* 19(1988):158−165; and my "Mystifications and mysteries in thought and research in educational administration," in G. S. Johnston and C. C. Yeakey, Eds., *Research and thought in administrative theory,* Lanham, MD: University Press of America, 1986. Simon discusses satisficing in his *Administrative behavior.* See two articles by C. E. Lindblom, both in *Public Administration*

Review, "The science of muddling through," 19(1959):79–88, and "Still muddling, not yet through," 39(1979):517–526.

[101] My papers are "The professorship in educational administration: A rationale," in D. J. Willower and J. A. Culbertson (Eds.), *The professorship in educational administration,* Columbus, OH and University Park, PA: University Council for Educational Administration and The Pennsylvania State University, 1964; and "Evolution in the professorship: Past, philosophy, future," *Educational Administration Quarterly,* 19(1983):179–200. The report on educational administration is, National Commission on Excellence in Educational Administration, *Leaders for America's schools,* Tempe, AZ: University Council for Educational Administration, 1987. The McCarthy study is McCarthy, Kuh, Newell and Iacona, *Under scrutiny: The educational administration professoriate.* Also see G. D. Kuh and M. M. McCarthy, "Key Actors in the Reform of Administrative Preparation Programs," *Planning and Changing,* 20(1989):108–126.

[102] R. F. Campbell's comments are in "The professorship in educational administration: A personal view." Some research suggests that study of a variety of theories can result in more sophisticated views of the world among educational administration students. See, for example, P. F. Silver and R. Hess, "The value of theory coursework in enhancing students' conceptual complexity," *Journal of Educational Administration,* 19(1981):11–20.

[103] Two recent papers on reflective methods in teaching educational administration are P. V. Bredeson, "Reappraising personal experience in the preparation of school administrators," *Journal of School Leadership,* 1(1991):176–189; N. A. Prestine and B. F. LeGrand, "Cognitive learning theory and the preparation of educational administrators," *Educational Administration Quarterly,* 27(1991):61–89. The first dealt with reflective methods as a vehicle to assess personal experience and the second discussed a theory of situated cognition which was seen as consistent with reflective practice. Joseph Licata and his colleagues have successfully used consequence analysis as described here and in earlier papers in projects designed to improve school problem solving in the States of Georgia and Louisiana. See J. W. Licata, "Consequence analysis: Theory and practice in school problem solving,"

Educational Technology, 18(1978):22−28, and "Learner perceptions of a clinical component for school administration," *Journal of Educational Systems Technology,* 9(1980−81):55−66; Licata and C. D. Ellett, "Lead program provides support, development for new principals," *NASSP Bulletin,* 74(1990):5−10.

[104] The studies are Campbell and Newell, *A study of professors of educational administration,* published in 1973; McCarthy, Kuh, Newell and Iacona, *Under scrutiny: The educational administration professoriate,* published in 1988; and J. C. Daresh, "The Professorship in Educational Administration: Emerging Trends," *Journal of Research and Development in Education,* 21(1988):22−29.

[105] National Commission on Excellence in Education, *Leaders for America's schools.*

[106] Truth on this view is contingent. Thus, Dewey's term for truth is warranted assertibility. Surprisingly, Habermas also adopted this term. See Dewey's, *Logic: The theory of inquiry*; and P. Pettit, "Habermas on Truth and Justice," in Parkinson, *Marx and Marxisms.*

[107] W. K. Hoy, C. J. Tarter, and R. B. Kottkamp, *Open schools, healthy schools.* Newbury Park, CA: Sage, 1991.

[108] In education, Wolcott's, *The man in the principal's office* is an example of anthropological field research, while H. S. Becker's, "The teacher in the authority system of the public school," *Journal of Educational Sociology,* 27(1953):128−141, is one of the earliest of the sociological genre; Anderson's "Critical ethnography in education," lumps neo-Marxists, feminists, and interpretivists under the critical ethnography label. This mixes quite different types; for instance, many feminist scholars are not only non-Marxist but anti-Marxist. It also ignores history, in particular, the use of the term critical theory to designate a version of Western Marxism, as cited earlier. See Held, *Introduction to critical theory,* p. 13. Microethnography is frequently concerned with language. See Green and Wallet, *Ethnography and language in educational settings.* The more rigorous approaches are emphasized in Owens, "Methodological rigor in naturalistic inquiry" and Lincoln and Guba, *Naturalistic inquiry.* The latter is an unusual book in that it is a combination of a superb treatment of the technology of observational research in which concepts from quantitative methods are

rendered in qualitative terms and an almost comically inept discussion of philosophical issues. As a work with this kind of split personality, it has received some highly negative reviews. For instance, one reviewer referred to it as "in essence an intellectually dishonest polemic." See K. Mazure, "Review of *Naturalistic Inquiry*," *Journal of Educational Thought*, 22(1988):57–63. In fairness, it should be said that, at least in my perception, this generalization was based mainly on Lincoln and Guba's philosophical commentary. Everhart, "Fieldwork methodology in educational administration" is a lucid review of qualitative work in educational administration. My own biases run to the sociological, having studied research methods with Alvin Gouldner at Buffalo when he was working on the project that led to his *Patterns of industrial bureaucracy*, Glencoe, IL: Free Press; and *Wildcat strike*, New York: Harper, both 1954. These biases are reflected in my first field study done in the early 1960s of a junior high school and the norms, attitudes, and behavior of various groups and individuals, especially what we called the school's teacher subculture. See my "The teacher subculture" in L. W. Drabek, *Interpreting education: A sociological approach*, New York: Appleton-Century-Crofts, 1971. This book reprints two of the earlier journal articles on the study. Almost thirty years later, I must confess that I still find a socio-cultural approach useful in field research and in understanding schools. I'm not sure if that means the concepts are durable or I'm intractable. In any case, it is well to be explicit about one's preferences or biases.

[109] For a brief statement about disputes in anthropology over ethnography see P. R. Sanday, "The ethnographic paradigm(s)," *Administrative Science Quarterly*, 24(1979):527–538. One of the most frequently cited sources on using field research to develop theory is B. G. Glaser and A. L. Strauss, *The discovery of grounded theory: Strategies for qualitative research*, Chicago: Aldine, 1967. Glaser and Strauss emphasize theory generation rather than verification, but insist that both are essential to the scientific enterprise.

[110] For an example of the debate in sociology in the 1930s see W. Waller, "Insight and scientific method," *American Journal of Sociology*, 40(1934):285–297. In the 1950s see M. Trow, "Comment on 'participant observation and interviewing: A comparison,'"

Human Organization, 16(1957):33−35. On ideology and field work, see Anderson, "Critical ethnography in education," and sources cited therein.

[111] These kinds of issues are discussed in R. M. Emerson, "Observational field work," *Annual Review of Sociology,* 7(1981):351−378.

[112] M. Hammersley, "From ethnography to theory," *Sociology,* 19(1985):244−259; G. V. Stimson, "Viewpoint: Place and space in sociological fieldwork," *The Sociological Review,* 34(1986):641−656. A study of props and space in educational administration is J. M. Lipham and D. C. Franke, "Non-verbal behavior of administrators," *Educational Administration Quarterly,* 2(1966):101−109.

[113] A choice that seems inappropriate is "naturalistic," which has been used mainly in education. The word naturalistic refers, of course, to a philosophic position. It is well established in that field as attested to in R. B. Winn, "Philosophic naturalism," in D. B. Runes (Ed.), *Twentieth century philosophy,* New York: Philosophical Library, 1947. To make matters worse, naturalism as a philosophy is not at all consistent with the positions taken by Lincoln and Guba, who titled their book on field research, *Naturalistic inquiry,* and appear to be at least one source for the use of the term in education.

[114] J. Wagner, "Administrators as ethnographers: School as a context for inquiry and action," *Anthropology and Education Quarterly,* 21(1990):195−221.

[115] On the importance of optimism in this context see J. T. Greer, "An optimist's view of educational administraton," *Journal of School Leadership,* 1(1991):7−18. See also S. H. Popper's criticism of the pessimism of a form of subjectivism as inappropriate for educational administration because of the need for optimism. "In dispraise of existential humanism in educational administration," *Educational Administration Quarterly,* 7(1971):26−50. The concept of the self-fulfilling prophecy is discussed in Merton, *Social theory and social structure.*

[116] The humanities can also play a part in teaching decision making. See S. H. Popper, *Pathways to the humanities in educational administration,* Tempe, AZ: University Council for Educational Administration, rev. ed., 1990. A number of persons have employed novels in this connection, for instance, R. E. Jennings, who was using them in his University at Buffalo classes in the 1970s.

[117] See, for example, "Evolution in the professorship," *Educational Administration Quarterly*.

[118] N. J. Smelser, "Introduction," in Smelser, *Handbook of sociology*, p. 11; Culbertson, "A century's quest for a knowledge base," p. 24; D. E. Griffiths, "Administrative theory," in Boyan, *Handbook of research on educational administration*. It might also be noted that the reviewer of Lincoln and Guba's *Naturalistic inquiry* stated that in discussing research procedures, those authors "at times appear indiscernible from the hardnosed 'scientists' of whom they are so contemptuous," Mazure, p. 61.

[119] The situation is reminiscent of the logocentric predicament which is based on the proposition that one cannot criticize logic without using it.

[120] The old saw about an irrational passion for dispassionate rationalism has some relevance, although I would deny that the label fits the position presented.

BIBLIOGRAPHIC ADDENDUM

A major new book on philosophy and educational administration is *Knowing educational administration* by C. W. Evers and G. Lakomski, London: Pergamon, 1991. This is a landmark work that goes beyond the articles by those authors cited above. The British journal, *Educational Management and Administration* devoted its July 1993 (Vol. 21, No. 3) issue to the book. It included articles by Evers and Lakomski, Bates, Hodgkinson, Gronn and Ribbins, and me.

C. Hodgkinson, *Educational leadership: The moral art,* Albany, NY: SUNY Press, 1991 is that author's third book on ethics in educational administration. It again presents a theory of value types with the top of the hierarchy representing principles with "a quality of absoluteness." The book is leavened with nuggets of the usual Hodgkinson wit and wisdom.

T. B. Greenfield and P. Ribbins are editors of *Greenfield on educational administration: Towards a humane science,* London: Routledge, 1993. This is a collection of the writings of Greenfield who died in 1992. The Gronn and Ribbins article in *Educational Management and Administration* is also useful in understanding Greenfield's thinking.

There appears to be a Dewey revival in at least some quarters. See, for example, E. Robertson, "Is Dewey's educational vision still viable?" in Volume 18 of the *Review of Research in Education* edited by G. Grant, Washington, D.C.: American Educational Research Association, 1992, and J. Garrison, "Realism, Deweyan pragmatism and educational research," *Educational Researcher,* 23, 1994, pp. 5–14. My "Dewey's theory of inquiry and reflective administration," *Journal of Educational Administration,* 32, 1994, pp. 5–22 presents the key ideas in Dewey's philosophy and discusses their applications in educational administration.

A new book on values in educational administration is L. G. Beck, *Reclaiming educational administration as a caring profession,* New York: Teachers College Press, 1994. As suggested by its title, the central theme of this work is caring. T. J. Sergiovanni, *Moral leadership*, San Francisco: Jossey-Bass, 1992, deals with ethical issues, especially as they relate to leadership.

The production of writing on field studies continues unabated. A thoughtful book not cited in the monograph is A. Strauss and J. Corbin, *Basics of qualitative research*, Newbury Park, CA: Sage, 1990. A related article by Corbin and Strauss is, "Grounded theory research: Procedures, canons and evaluative criteria," *Qualitative Sociology*, 13, 1990, pp. 3–21.

Both the *Encyclopedia of educational research* (1992) and the *International encyclopedia of education* (1994) appeared after the monograph was published. My entries in each are written from the perspective used here. These compilations should be scanned for pieces that add something to the topics discussed. To cite one example from *EER*, E. E. Ericson, "Philosophical issues in education," provides insights into directions in educational philosophy and the contemporary blending of different approaches taking place in that field.

A surprising amount of writing in educational administration (and education generally) on philosophical questions and the social sciences continues to be sadly uninformed. An example is the confusion about functionalism. One writer recently called Frederick W. Taylor of scientific management fame a leading functionalist scholar. Another described "functionalist ethical criteria" as if that sociological theory had been explicitly presented as a moral philosophy. Some align functionalism with its enemy, positivism. This sort of thing reflects the lack of preparation in philosophy and the social sciences of too many professors, as well as the turn toward advocacy by some that can result in lumping truly diverse views in a large category made up of those outside the circle of believers. Educational administration also continues to exhibit the faddism that has marked all of education over the years. Two of the latest panaceas, both reasonable in some respects, but rife with potential negative consequences, are total quality management and multicultural education. Clearly, the need for openminded skepticism and thoughtful inquiry is more critical than ever.

INDEX

ADORNO, T. W., 6, 15
ALEXANDER, J. C., 21
BATES, R. J., 8
BLASE, J., 14
BLUMER, H., 5
BOYAN, N. J., 2
BURRELL, G., 17
CAMPBELL, R. F., 47, 48
CLARK, D. L., 40
COLLINS, R., 30–31
Committee for the Advancement of School Administration, 1
Cooperative Program in Educational Administration, 1
Critical theory, 6–11, 18–19, 21, 23–24
    see also Marxism and neo-Marxism,
CULBERTSON, J., 44, 60
DARESH, J. C., 48
Decision making, 38–41, 43, 55, 57
Deconstruction, 15–16
Deliberation, 41ff.
DERRIDA, J., 15
DEWEY, J., 24, 34, 37, 41ff., 59
    principles, 71, 74, 76
Dialectical methods, 28–29
DILTHEY, W., 11, 30
Existentialism, 5, 11, 12
Field studies, 2, 6, 8, 13, 14–15, 19, 26–27, 52–54, 76, 77, 78
FOSTER, W., 7–8
FOUCOULT, M., 15
Frankfurt School, 6–7, 10
Functionalism, 8, 17
GARFINKEL, H., 5
Gender, 6, 16, 22, 48–49

GIROUX, H. A., 10
GOULDNER, A. W., 7
GREENFIELD, T. B., 6, 12ff., 20, 23, 25, 39
GRIFFITH, D. E., 22, 60
GRONN, P., 15
HABERMAS, J., 6, 7, 76
HAMMERSLEY, M., 53
HART, A. W., 14–15
HARTLEY, H. J., 12
HEAP, J. L., 11
HEGEL, G. W. F., 29
HEISENBERG, W., 15
HELD, D., 19
Hermeneutics, 5, 11, 29–30, 71
HODGKINSON, C., 13, 14, 20
HORKHEIMER, M., 6, 7
HOY, W. K., 50
HUSSERL, E., 11, 12, 29, 71
Idealism, 11
In-basket study, 39
Inquiry, 23, 24–32
    values, 34–44ff., 50–53, 55–57, 59–60
    see also science
Inquiry in educational administration, 1–4, 21–27, 49–54, 59–60
Journals in educational administration, 2
KANT, I., 29, 33
KUHN, T. S., 15, 67
LAKOMSKI, G., 20
LINDBLOM, C., 44
Logic-in-use, 40
Logocentric predicament, 79
MANNING, P. K., 5
MARCUSE, H., 6

83

MARTINDALE, D., 17
MARX, K., 6, 22, 29
Marxism and neo-Marxism, 4–7, 8–11, 18–19, 21–22, 24–25, 27, 29–31, 52–53, 68, 69
  see also critical theory
MCCARTHY, M. M., 45, 48
MCLAREN, P., 10
MEAD, G. H., 5, 42
MORGAN, G., 17
Muddling through, 44
National Commission on Excellence in Educational Administration, 48
National Council of Professors of Educational Administration, 1, 3
Naturalism, 70, 78
New sociology of education, 7
NEWELL, L. J., 48
NIETZSCHE, F., 15
Organizational culture, 42–44
PARSONS, T., 17
Phenomenology, 11–12, 29–30
  M. Farber, 71
PLATO, 33
Positivism, 8, 12, 16–17, 20, 25, 30, 32, 34, 71
Postmodernism, 15–16
Pragmatism, 5, 18, 24, 70
Praxis and practice, 9–10, 23–24, 38–44, 45–48, 55, 59
Professors of educational administration, 5, 44–57
Race and ethnicity, 16
Reflective methods, 24, 34, 39, 41, 59, 74, 75, 81
  internalization, 42, 55
  institutionalization, 42–44

Reflexiveness, 42
RICKMAN, H. P., 30
RORTY, R., 30
ROTH, P. A., 11
Satisficing, 44
SCHELER, M., 11
SCHUTZ, A., 5
Science, 4–5, 16, 23, 24–28, 30–32, 49–54, 59–60
  norms of, 25–27
  see also inquiry
SIMON, H. A., 8, 13, 40, 44
SMELZER, N. J., 5, 59–60
Social class, 5, 6–8, 18–19, 22
Social sciences, 20, 21, 25, 26–27, 31–32
  attacks on, 4–8, 12–13, 15–16
  in educational administration, 1–4, 49–54
Sociology, 3, 23, 30–31, 59–60
  trends in, 21
SOCRATES, 42
STIMSON, G. V., 53
Subjectivism, 4–6, 11–15, 19–20, 23
Symbolic interactionism, 5, 12, 14, 53
Teaching educational administration, 45–48, 55–56
University Council for Educational Administration, 1
Values, 3, 5, 13–14, 16, 23–24, 32–37
VANDENBERG, D., 11
VIERKANDT, A., 11
WALLER, W., 8
WALLERSTEIN, I., 5
WARNER, W. L., 6
WILLIS, P., 9, 26–27, 31
WOLCOTT, H. F., 26

ABOUT THE AUTHOR

DONALD J. WILLOWER is distinguished professor of education at The Pennsylvania State University where he has also chaired the educational administration program, been acting dean of the College of Education, and twice been acting head of the Division of Education Policy Studies. He holds three degrees from the University at Buffalo, the B.A. and M.A., both in philosophy and an Ed.D. in general administration. He worked in private sector management, served in the Buffalo Public Schools, and was a Kellogg Fellow at the University of Oregon.

He was a member of the American Association of School Administrators' National Commission on the Professional Preparation of School Administrators and the University Council for Educational Administration's National Commission on Excellence in Educational Administration. He also served as UCEA president.

Twice winner of Davis Awards for best publication in *Educational Administration Quarterly,* he is author or coauthor of about 160 publications that deal mainly with schools as organizations and philosophical issues in educational administration. Most of his more than eighty doctoral graduates hold positions in public schools or universities.